SECOND EDITION

# A Year of
# Living
## WITH MORE
# COMPASSION

**52** Quotes & Weekly
Compassion Practices

*Published by:*
FACES Conferences
4510 N. Flecha Drive
Tucson, AZ 85718
1.877.63FACES
www.facesconferences.com

ISBN 978-0-985-4979-1-0

"Love and compassion
are necessities, not luxuries.
Without them humanity
cannot survive."

*His Holiness the Dalai Lama*

SECOND EDITION

# A Year of Living

## WITH MORE
## COMPASSION

# 52 Quotes & Weekly Compassion Practices

Richard Fields, PhD – Editor

*Published by FACES Conferences*
*Tucson, AZ*
www.facesconferences.com

*This book is dedicated to the memory of my*

*wonderful mother, Libby Fields*

A special thanks and gratitude to all our teachers
who contributed to this 2nd edtion.

Thanks to Jack Kornfield and Tara Brach for embracing
the mission of this book and for their support.

A special thanks to Chris Germer and Kristin Neff for their inspiration,
suggestions, and commitment to making this book a reality.

Of course, our gratitude to our talented designer
Don Stayner (www.dsdwerx.com), whose commitment to this project
is so elegantly reflected in these pages.

Table of Contents

## SECTION I ▪ *Self-Compassion*
### *QUOTES NO. 1–8*

## SECTION II ▪ *Compassion Readiness*
### *QUOTES NO. 9–15*

# SECTION V ▪ *A Better Way to Deal with Reactive Emotions: Anger, Hate, Criticism, Fear*
## *QUOTES NO. 29–37*

# SECTION VI ▪ *Opening Your Heart: Kindness, Generosity & Forgiveness*
## *QUOTES NO. 38–42*

## SECTION VII ▪ *Compassion & Suffering*
### *QUOTES NO. 43–52*

## APPENDIX

The quotes and write-ups we received from our teachers,
while all independent of each other, touch on several
overlapping themes. They are organized into seven sections.

### A Year of Living with More Compassion:
### 52 Quotes & Weekly Compassion Practices, 2nd Edition

Section I – *Self-Compassion*   Quotes No. 1-8

Section II – *Compassion Readiness*   Quotes No. 9-15

Section II – *Opening Your Compassionate Heart*   Quotes No. 16-20

Section IV – *Compassion & Connection*   Quotes No. 21-28

Section V – *A Better Way to Deal with Reactive Emotions:*
*Anger, Hate, Criticism, Fear*   Quotes No. 29-37

Section VI – *Opening Your Heart: Kindness,*
*Generosity & Forgiveness*   Quotes No. 29-43

Section VII – *Compassion & Suffering*   Quotes No. 44-52

## *More Compassion In Your Life*

This handbook of compassion quotes, lessons, and practices is designed to help you increase your capacity for self-compassion and compassion for others. This second edition contains new quotes, and the best quotes from *A Year of Living More Mindfully: 52 Mindfulness Quotes & Practices* (2011), and the first edition of *A Year of Living with More Compassion: 52 Compassion Quotes & Practices*, (2012).

This second edition is redesigned and sequenced to more effectively build your capacity for self-compassion and compassion.

## *Why 52 Quotes?*

We have 52 quotes so you have one quote to work with for each week of the year. The Buddha habitually numbered things – the 4 noble truths, the 8-fold path. In that tradition we chose 52 Quotes for our format.

## *Our Teachers*

The twenty-eight teachers, leaders, and clinicians in the fields of mindfulness, compassion, and psychology, are very gifted, talented and remarkably people. Their wisdom, creativity, insights, lessons, and compassion practices, in our book, create a multifaceted approach to help you develop more compassion in your life.

## *How To Use This Book*

There are many ways to use this book. It is suggested that you focus on one compassion quote and practice per week. You might display the quote for the week on your computer, or on your cell phone, or even on your kitchen refrigerator (always a good place to remember to be self-compassionate).

You might also choose to memorize the compassion quote for that week, and keep it in your consciousness. You can then follow the compassion practice for that week for that quote.

**Other suggestions:**
Keeping a journal is also helpful. One or more times a week write down any observations, awareness, feelings, and intentions that might arise. You might also notice any resistance to certain quotes and practices, as well as, any preferences.

Notice that each quote, lesson, and practice has some bold type. This is intended to remind you of the **key points** for that quote and make it easier to review without reading the entire write-up. Some people have found it helpful to first read the whole section, before starting to focus on the first quote in that section. The book is organized in a sequence that builds upon each section. For the full impact we suggest you **start with section I and then continue quote by quote until you finish with section VII.**

These are just suggestions for using this book. Feel free to use the book as you see fit. Maybe you will skip through the book concentrating on particular quotes and practices. You may choose to randomly flip through the book and pick a quote and practice that you would like to work on.

## Mission

The hope and mission of the book is to help you achieve more self-compassion and compassion, by shifting away from blame, criticism self-limiting habits. The result will be more compassion in your life, better relationships and connection, and a stronger sense of well-being. Enjoy!

## Why Compassion is Important

Compassion is nothing new. It has a long and noble history. It's at the core of all the world's religions and hardwired into our DNA. Confucius said, "Never do to others what you would not like them to do to you." Charles Darwin observed that "those communities, which included the greatest number of the most sympathetic members, would flourish best."

Over the last few years, there has been a burgeoning scientific interest in compassion that is changing our understanding of it. There is new recognition that compassion is good for you – *very* good for you, being closely related to happiness, wisdom, emotional resilience, better relationships, improved health, and a host of other factors.

**Compassion is a *strength* that allows us to transform emotional suffering, it is a *skill* that can be learned, and it can be *directed toward oneself.*** Brain scans are demonstrating that compassion activates pleasure centers even in the presence of suffering, transforming pain for the better. But a warmhearted response to suffering may not automatically arise in us, especially when we feel frightened by it. Compassion training can help us develop the skill of compassion through deliberate mental practice, changing the brain for the better even after only a few weeks of practicing methods such as those described in this book. Finally, our new, scientifically-informed model of compassion indicates that we can give compassion to ourselves when we need it the most. Cultivating a warm, connected presence with ourselves provides a basis for our capacity to be compassionate to others.

The current interest in compassion seems to be the next step in the unprecedented convergence of ancient Buddhist psychology and practice with modern scientific psychology. The first step was mindfulness, which may be considered the foundation of compassion. Our emerging reinterpretation of compassion is starting to transform, albeit still in small ways, how we approach mental health, education, parenting, and areas of our professional life. It's becoming a new meme – a transmittable cultural idea. This change cannot come soon enough, however, if we reflect even for a moment on the complex challenges facing humanity today.

The 52 quotes in this book, their interpretations, and the compassion practices are a beautiful blend of the old and the new. Many of the contributors are currently evolving our modern understanding of compassion and they share here some of their own inspirations. They also offer simple, yet profound suggestions for actualizing the benefits of compassion in our own lives. **If you allow this book to be a bedside companion for the next year, your life may never be the same.**

*Christopher Germer, PhD*
*Coeditor,* Wisdom and Compassion in Psychotherapy, *2012*

## Quotes №1 to 8

# Self-Compassion

"Caring for others, requires caring for oneself."
*His Holiness the Dalai Lama*

QUOTE #1 – Germer
*Self-Compassion Increases our Capacity for Compassion for Others*

QUOTE #2 – Neff
*Self-Acceptance: Quieting the Self-Critic*

QUOTE #3 – Gilbert
*A Friendly Compassionate Voice*

QUOTE #4 – Neff
*Putting Personal Inadequacies (Our Own Darkness) in Perspective*

QUOTE #5 – Shapiro
*Loneliness and "The Trance of Unworthiness"*

QUOTE #6 – Weintraub
*Self-Compassion: Quieting the "inner Critic"*

QUOTE #7 – Shaprio
*Self-Compassion & Self-Love*

QUOTE #8 – Neff
*Accessing Natural Self-Compassion*

CHRIS GERMER, PhD, chose this quote:

**66**

For someone to develop genuine
compassion towards others,
first he or she must have a basis
upon which to cultivate compassion,
and that basis is the ability
to connect to one's own feelings
and to care for one's own welfare...
**Caring for others requires
caring for oneself.**

**99**

*His Holiness the Dalai Lama,*
www.dalailama.com/teachings/training-the-mind/verse-7,
excerpted from, Transforming the Mind, *2000*

**THEME** – *Self-Compassion Increases our Capacity for Compassion for Others*

Self-compassion is a healthy response to one's own suffering, much as we'd respond to someone whom we truly love. As the Dalai Lama points out, it's the foundation of caring for others, for how can we cherish in others what we find distasteful in ourselves.

There are a variety of misunderstandings about self-compassion that interfere with giving ourselves the kindness we need. For example, self-compassion is often confused with self-indulgence, self-pity, or self-absorption. The research shows precisely the opposite. Self-compassion is unrelated to narcissism and self-compassionate people tend to feel more connected and compassionate toward others. **Furthermore, turning toward ourselves with kindness when we suffer, fail, or feel inadequate decreases anxiety and depression and enhances emotional resilience.**

Why the persistent bias against self-compassion, even among Buddhist scholars? The underlying fear seems to be that the "self" in self-compassion subtly reinforces the illusion of separation. The Buddha was very clear that "selfing" is the cause of most emotional suffering. We spend our entire lives promoting and protecting our "selves" against real or imagined danger, entirely missing the miracle of life unfolding in and around us. For example, neuroimaging research demonstrates that the brain reverts to a "default mode" when it's in a resting state, which typically means rumination about personal problems that occurred in the past or could occur in the future. We certainly don't want to add any practices to our lives that compound our suffering by strengthening the sense of a fixed, separate self. Which begs the question: "When should we direct compassion toward ourselves and when toward others?"

The litmus test of self-compassion seems to be whether it leads to more or less "selfing." **If a warm, tender attitude toward ourselves decreases rumination and allows us to connect with others, it's probably a good thing. When we feel reasonably good, then focusing on the needs of others might provide still greater emotional freedom and joy.**

### COMPASSION PRACTICE FOR THE WEEK

*Set your mind to be aware when you're under stress, perhaps 3-4 times per day. When stress occurs, put your hand over your heart and say to yourself, "May I be happy and free from suffering." Notice how you feel. Then focus on a person who may be involved in your stressful situation, put your hand over your heart and say, "May you be happy and free from suffering." How do you feel now? Note which practice brought you the most emotional freedom.*

*"May I be happy and free from suffering."*
*"May you be happy and free from suffering."*

KRISTIN NEFF, PhD, chose this quote:

# The curious paradox is that when I accept myself just as I am, then I can change.

*Carl Rogers,* On Becoming a Person: A Therapist's View of Psychotherapy, *1961*

## THEME – *Self-Acceptance: Quieting the Self-Critic*

I come back to this quote again and again because it so nicely captures the paradoxical nature of growth that occurs by practicing self-compassion. Many people are puzzled by the idea that we should accept ourselves as we are. Why? I'm a mess! Why would I want to accept myself? I want to change, and need to criticize myself in order to do so.

**Self-criticism is not a useful motivator of change. Research shows that self-critics are much more likely to be anxious and depressed – mind states that can interfere with taking the steps needed for change.** Self-critics also have less self-confidence, which undermines their potential for success. The habit of self-criticism engenders fear of failure, meaning that self-critics often don't even try to achieve their goals because the possibility of failure is unacceptable. Even more problematic, self-critics have a hard time seeing themselves clearly and identifying needed areas of improvement because they know the self-punishment that will ensue if they admit the truth. Much better to deny there's a problem or, even better, blame it on someone else.

But is a compassionate response to our shortcomings any better? Yes.

It's relatively easy to see when we think about how a compassionate and caring parent might motivate a child who is struggling. Let's say your teenage daughter Mary comes home from school with a failing math grade. If you say, "You're so stupid and lame! What a loser! You're hopeless and will never amount to any-thing!" is that really going to help motivate Mary? Instead it will probably de-press her to the point of wanting to give up math all together. Much more effec-tive would be to take an understanding and supportive approach: "I know you're disappointed, and clearly something is not working in your study routine. But I know you can do it. How can I help and support you?" This compassionate approach is much more likely to give Mary the emotional resources needed to pick herself up and try again.

It's exactly the same when we take a caring and compassionate approach with ourselves. Compassion is concerned with the alleviation of suffering. When we feel compassion for our own pain – especially when the pain comes from our maladaptive habits and behaviors – we want to heal our pain. We want to make changes and improvements that will help us suffer less. **Self-compassion also allows us to more clearly acknowledge areas of personal weakness by recog-nizing that imperfection is part of the shared human experience.** We can then work on improving ourselves, not because we're unacceptable as we are, but because we want to thrive and be happy.

*Here's an exercise that can help you motivate change with self-acceptance rather than self-judgment.*

**1.** *Think about a personal trait for which you harshly criticize yourself (such as being negative, moody, overweight, etc.) and that you would like to change.*

**2.** *Try to get in touch with the emotional pain that your self-criticism causes, giving yourself compassion for the experience of feeling so judged. Remind yourself that you're only human, imperfect, just like the rest of us, with weakness as well as strengths.*

**3.** *Put your hand over your heart and repeat the phrase "May I be kind to myself. May I accept myself as I am."*

**4.** *Next, ask yourself what would a caring friend, parent, or partner say to gently encourage you to make a change, while also reminding you of their unconditional love and acceptance? What is the most supportive message this person could give you?*

**5.** *Put your hand over your heart again and repeat these words of caring encouragement to yourself.*

**"May I be kind to myself.
May I accept myself as I am."**

**You'll be much more likely to blossom
by watering the seeds of self-acceptance
rather than of self-criticism.**

# 3

PAUL GILBERT, PhD, chose this quote:

# I never beat myself up gently.

*Patient's saying*

## THEME – *A Friendly Self-Compassionate Voice*

Many years ago, when I was practicing therapy, I discovered that the way people tried to help themselves was often to be critical, harsh, and even bullying. "Come on, you idiot, stop thinking this way. Pull yourself together. You're making things worse. You're making mountains out of molehills. You should know better than this, etc." So I developed a very simple intervention to help people create an internal, kind voice. **If you practice every day hearing your own voice in your head (as you do when you think), textured with understanding, kindness, and support, this will help you in your times of difficulty.**

## COMPASSION PRACTICE FOR THE WEEK

*Sit quietly in a chair for a moment and slow the breath*
*to prepare the body. Now, for about 15-30 seconds*
*just stay with the facial expression you have right now,*
*which is probably neutral. Notice how that feels –*
*pay attention to your facial muscles. Then, for 15-30 seconds*
*create a friendly facial expression, as if you're with somebody*
*you really like being with – a kind of joyful friendliness.*
*Then go back to a neutral face for 15-30 seconds*
*and then back to a friendly face, so that you've done*
*each exercise twice. Reflect and compare and contrast*
*what happens to your body and your feelings*
*when you deliberately change facial expressions.*
*What did you notice? What happens if you sit for a while*
*just slowing the breath gently and focusing on a gentle,*
*friendly facial expression – nothing too exaggerated*
*or forced, just very gentle?*

*Next, we're going to generate a friendly thinking tone.*
*On the out- breath simply say "hello" to yourself –*
*and name yourself. So in my case it would be, "Hello Paul."*
*Do this for about 15-30 seconds on the out- breath*
*with a neutral tone in your voice. It is a "hello" that is*
*relatively indifferent – sort of factual. Notice how it feels.*
*Then, for the same amount of time, create a friendly voice,*
*as if you are speaking to somebody you really like being with*
*and are expressing your friendliness to him/her.*

It's a very welcoming tone. Practice different kinds of voices, until you get one that sounds really friendly and supportive and comfortable. Then, go back to neutral voice for about 15-30 seconds and notice what happens to your feelings. Finally, finish with a friendly voice. Now, for the next minute or two, practice just sitting with this idea of the inner friendly and compassionate voice.

Try to practice this every day for at least a minute – longer if you can – generating compassionate expressions and voice tones. The point here is to remember that this is important to do. So even if you practice for just a minute each day, at least you have acknowledged each day that paying attention to the emotional tone and textures of your thinking is very important. Note if your thoughts tend towards ruminating about things that anger you, if they take on an angry tone or maybe an anxious tone. When you think about yourself, what is the emotional tone of your thoughts? Try to create, on purpose, friendly, supportive, and wise tones. If you are troubled, spend a moment to slow the breath and ground the body and bring your compassionate inner voice to this moment.

KRISTIN NEFF, PhD, chose this quote:

> "
>
> Compassion is not a relationship between the healer and the wounded. It's a relationship between equals. Only when we know our own darkness well can we be present with the darkness of others. Compassion becomes real when we recognize our shared humanity.
>
> "

*Pema Chödrön,* The Places That Scare You: A Guide to Fearlessness in Difficult Times, *2001*

**THEME – *Putting Personal Inadequacies (Our Own Darkness) in Perspective***

One of the most important elements of self-compassion is the recognition of our shared humanity. Compassion is, by definition, relational. **Compassion literally means "to suffer with,"** which implies a basic mutuality in the experience of suffering. The emotion of compassion springs from the recognition that the human experience is imperfect, that we are all fallible. **When we're in touch with our common humanity, we remember that feelings of inadequacy and disappointment are universal.** This is what distinguishes self-compassion from self-pity. While self-pity says "poor me," self-compassion recognizes that suffering is part of the shared human experience. The pain I feel in difficult times is the same pain that you feel in difficult times. The triggers are different, the circumstances are different, the degree of pain is different, but the basic experience is the same.

Recognizing common humanity also allows us to be more understanding and less judgmental about our inadequacies. Our thoughts, feelings, and actions are largely impacted by factors outside of our control: parenting history, culture, genetic and environmental conditions, as well as the demands and expectations of others. After all, if we had full control over our behavior, how many people would consciously choose to have anger problems, addiction issues, debilitating social anxiety, or an eating disorder? Many aspects of our selves and the circumstances of our lives are not of our own choosing, but instead stem from innumerable factors that are outside our sphere of influence. When we acknowledge this reality, our difficulties do not have to be taken so personally. We can embrace ourselves and others with compassion, rather than blame.

## COMPASSION PRACTICE FOR THE WEEK

*Think about a trait that you often judge yourself for, and that is an important part of your self-definition. For example, you may think of yourself as a shy person, lazy, angry, etc. Then ask yourself the following questions:*

**1.** *How often do you display this trait – most of the time, sometimes, only occasionally? Who are you when you don't display the trait – are you still you?*

**2.** *Are you the only person who displays this trait, or is this a common human experience?*

**3.** *What are the various causes and conditions that led to having the trait in the first place (early family experiences, genetics, life pressures, etc.)? If these "outside" forces were partly responsible for you having this trait, is it accurate to think of the trait as reflecting the inner you?*

**4.** *What happens when you reframe your self-description so that you are not defining yourself in terms of the trait? For example, instead of saying, "I am an angry person," what happens when you say, "sometimes, in certain circumstances, I get angry." By identifying less strongly with this trait, does anything change? Can you sense any more space, freedom, and peace of mind?*

SHAUNA SHAPIRO, PhD, chose this quote:

"

# The bud stands for all things, even for those things that don't flower, for everything flowers, from within, of self-blessing; though sometimes it is necessary to reteach a thing its loveliness, to put a hand on its brow of the flower and retell it in words and in touch it is lovely until it flowers again from within, of self-blessing...

"

*Galway Kinell,* Saint Francis and the Sow, *1993*

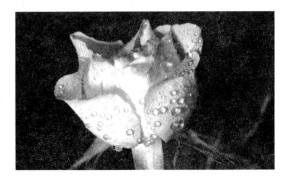

## THEME – *Loneliness and "The Trance of Unworthiness"*

In "Sir Frances and the Sow," the American poet Galway Kinnell reminds of us the power of self-blessing and of learning to trust our own loveliness.

One of the themes essential to mindfulness practice is the teaching of one's own basic goodness, our essential nature. And yet, one of the first things practitioners notice as we begin to pay attention to the patterns of mind and heart is how critical and judgmental we are of ourselves.

There is often a pervading sense that "I am not enough": "I am not good, kind, patient, smart, beautiful, generous…enough." **Most of the time, we are unconscious of this constant internal monologue of self-doubt and self-judgment, and yet this way of relating to ourselves is one of the greatest harms to our health, vitality and well being.**

Author and mindfulness teacher Tara Brach refers to this as "the trance of unworthiness," which imprisons us in an illusion of separateness and pain, distorting our view of ourselves and of life. **When left unnoticed, this trance of unworthiness can become the automatic lens through which life is viewed, leading to fear, dissatisfaction and a sense of aloneness.** By inclining our mind toward self-care and self-blessing, we can begin to loosen the self-destructive patterns and cultivate compassion, care, kindness and friendliness for ourselves.

We begin to notice how we relate to ourselves, the tone of voice we use to speak to ourselves, the words we say, how we care for ourselves. We begin to see how significantly the way we relate to ourselves colors our perception and we realize that carrying around these negative views and expectations is a burden preventing us from being truly present for ourselves, for others and for life.

## COMPASSION PRACTICE FOR THE WEEK

**1.** *Each morning when you awaken, set a clear intention to be kind to yourself today.*

**2.** *Begin to notice the number of times each day you judge or criticize yourself. How does it feel in your body when you notice this?* **Be careful not to judge yourself for judging. Simply notice, and then make a choice to let the judgment go, returning to your intention of self-kindness.**

**3.** *Practice saying three kind, acknowledging statements to yourself each day. They can be simple, e.g. "I am grateful that I ate a nutritious lunch today," or, "I was really present for my son this morning." What is most important is not the content of what you say but the process of beginning a new pattern of speaking to yourself with kindness.*

**4.** *Practice "self-blessing" each night before bed. For example, "May I be peaceful," "May I be safe and protected," "May I be healthy," "May I be happy." You may use any of these phrases or choose phrases that feel most nourishing to you.* **Through these practices you are beginning to re-teach yourself your own loveliness.**

# 6

AMY WEINTRAUB, MFA, ERYT-500, chose this quote:

**" My beloved Child, break your heart no longer. Each time you judge yourself you break your own heart. "**

*Swami Kripalvananda*

# THEME – *Self-Compassion: Quieting the "Inner Critic"*

How many hundreds of yoga classes did I teach, quoting my teacher at the end of each class, before my heart's mind understood those words? Why did saying them to my students still bring tears to my eyes? Why, after years of meditation, therapy, and medication, was I still so mean to myself? Before I began a daily yoga practice in the late 1980s, no amount of meditation turned the volume down on that monster in my mind. Every one of us has an inner critic. Mark Twain said that if we talked to our children the way we talk to ourselves, we would be arrested for child abuse. I was particularly hard on myself in the 1970s after my marriage failed. Had anyone been listening to my self-abuse, they would have locked me up and thrown away the key.

My secret name for myself was "Amy Shamey." **Shame wasn't just a thought or belief. It wasn't just an emotion. It was a part of my physical being, a daily visceral experience that whooshed through my body, bringing waves of heat, a feeling of humiliation and with it, grief.** No amount of talking about it in therapy, watching it arise on the meditation cushion, or numbing it out with meds, touched the core of my self-hatred. Of course, my body image had a lot to do with it. I saw myself as chubby, unattractive, and clumsy, compared to my beautiful mother, whose expressive face appeared on the covers of magazines like *True Confessions* and *Romance* in the late 1940s. My body was not my friend. It had an embarrassing plumpness in the places that should have been lean and an embarrassing flatness in the places that should have been round. From this description, you might think I wasn't pretty. We're talking about self-image here, not reality. Pictures attest to my cuteness as a kid and my downright beauty in my teens. I don't think my creative dance teacher would have tried to convince my mother when I was eleven to enroll me in a proper ballet studio with daily classes if she hadn't seen in me a grace and fluidity I couldn't see in myself. But whatever the source, I hated my body and nearly everything else that went by the name of Amy.

So what changed? In the late 1980s, I made my first visit to Kripalu Center in Stockbridge, Massachusetts and took my first yoga class. Despite meditating since the early 1970s and practicing a bit of yoga asana, it wasn't until that first visit to Kripalu that a teacher spoke the words attributed to Swami Kripalvananda, "My beloved child, break your heart no longer. Each time you judge yourself, you break your own heart." I am sure I wept on my mat when I heard them, although I don't remember. What I do remember is emerging from the class feeling a sense of spacious abundance, a touching into wholeness that I had never experienced before. In those moments after class, it didn't matter what I looked like or what mistakes I may have made in my life. I had touched something deep within me that was absolutely perfect, just as it was. In those moments after class, there was nothing I needed to fix, no way I needed to change.

I left Kripalu with a commitment to practicing yoga every day. After each morning of stretching and breathing and staying present to the physical sensations the poses evoked, I felt more at home in my body. I rose from my mat feeling at ease with the Amy who looked back at me from the mirror.

The self-judgment didn't immediately cease in the hours I spent off the mat, but eventually the daily whoosh of shame became weekly, then monthly, and then it disappeared altogether. If my inner critic attacked, I found myself talking back instead of believing everything she said. When I rolled out my mat to practice, her voice fell silent. When I made a mistake or fell short of my own expectations, she always had something to say, but I didn't necessarily believe her anymore. By the early 1990s, I was teaching a workshop at Kripalu called *Befriending Your Inner Critic*, leading others in exercises to find compassion for themselves, including their shame parts and their nasty inner critics. From that workshop, I offer you a compassion practice.

## COMPASSION PRACTICE

*Spend a week with this compassion practice and watch your compassion for all your parts begin to outshine the weakening voice of your inner critic. Part One is a practice of breathing while moving that, in addition to bringing in more fresh oxygen and releasing old carbon dioxide from your lungs, provides an opportunity to be fully aware of and be present to physical sensations. This sensory awareness is the portal into the moving meditation we will do in Part Two that offers compassion to places in your body. You can do each practice by itself, but it works best to put them together.*

### Part One: Power Hara Breath

1. *Stand with your feet slightly wider than hip width apart and bring hands to your shoulders with your elbows pointed out like chicken wings.*

2. *Inhale, filling your lungs halfway as you twist to the left.*

3. *Inhale fully as you twist to the right.*

4. *Extend your right arm forcefully to the left as you twist to the left, exhaling through your mouth with a vigorous "ha" sound.*

5. *Extend your left arm forcefully to the right as you twist to the right, exhaling again through your mouth with a "ha" sound.*

6. *Practice five to ten full rounds. Release and stand with your eyes closed and your palms open. Sense deeply into your face, feel the sensation in your face, your arms, the palms of your hands. Sense the tingling in your palms.*

**Part Two: "Be still beloved, and know that you are safely held."**

1. *Let your right hand nest in your left hand with the tips of your thumbs touching and say to yourself, "Be still, beloved hands and know that you are safely held."*

2. *Bounce on your feet for about thirty seconds. Stop and feel the sensation in your feet. Say to yourself, "Be still, beloved feet and know that you are safely held."*

3. *Now find a comfortable seated position or lie down on the floor. Repeat the phrase, moving through your body, like this: "Be still beloved (body part)," as you inhale; "and know that you are safely held," as you exhale.*

4. *Begin with the left foot. "Be still beloved left foot," as you inhale; "and know that you are safely held," as you exhale. Repeat this phrase as you move up the left side of your body, all the way up to your crown. As you speak to your head, you might wish to place your hands on your head so your little fingers are touching at your hairline and your index fingers point to your crown.*

5. *Do the same practice, beginning with the right foot and moving up the right side of your body.*

6. *Speak to your torso, including your buttocks, genitals, belly, chest, spine, and breasts. Feel free to place your hands on each body part as you speak to it.*

*End by placing your right hand on your heart, and your left hand on top, linking your thumbs in a hand gesture called eagle mudra. End with the phrase,* **"Be still beloved heart, and know that you are safely held."**

## 7

SHAUNA L. SHAPIRO, PhD, chose this quote:

> You can search
> throughout the entire
> universe for someone
> who is more deserving of
> your love and affection
> than you are yourself.

*The Buddha*

## THEME – *Self-Compassion & Self-Love*

**In this quote the Buddha offers the radical teaching that each of us is deserving of self-compassion and self-love.** We are often taught that it is important to have compassion and to love thy neighbor as thyself. And yet, when we look closely at our own "self-compassion" and "self-love" we often find it is painfully lacking. Some years ago, one of my teachers invited me to reflect deeply on my relationship to myself. She asked, "Do you love yourself? Do you have compassion for yourself?" And when I reflected upon this I was unsure. She suggested that I begin to say each day, "I love you Shauna. I have compassion for you, Shauna," and to try to feel and embody this. I looked at her as if she were crazy, and flat out said, "No, that's not the practice for me. It feels too forced and airy-fairy and I'm not sure it is authentic." She gently conceded, and offered a different practice, "How about simply saying, "Good morning, Shauna."

"Yes" I replied, "that I can do." I had recently divorced and I would often wake up in the morning feeling sad and alone. Now, when I woke up, I began to say, "Good morning, Shauna," and I felt the kindness and self-compassion in this simple morning greeting. After a few months, my teacher asked how the good morning practice was going. I shared how natural it had become and that I was actually enjoying it. "It sounds like you have graduated," she responded with a soft smile. "Your next practice is to say, "Good morning, I love and have compassion for you, Shauna."

And then one morning, I felt "it." I actually felt love and compassion for myself pouring through me. Tears filled my eyes as I poignantly realized that I was experiencing self-love and self-compassion for the first time that I could remember. I felt so vulnerable and raw. I also felt so grateful and so alive.

I would like to say these feelings of self-love and self-compassion now pervade my every moment of lived experience and that I float through life encapsulated in a soft white light of unconditional self-love and self-compassion. This is not the case. However, I can say that the pattern of self-love and self-compassion, once created, has never ceased to exist. It is something I can return to and remember over and over again. The American author and physician Oliver Wendell Holmes wrote that **"a mind once stretched...never regains its original dimensions." I would add that a heart once stretched never regains it original dimensions.**

## COMPASSION PRACTICE FOR THE WEEK

**1.** *Reflect upon the Buddha's teaching:*

*"You can search throughout the entire universe*
*for someone who is more deserving of your love*
*and affection than you are yourself."*

*Do you believe this? What would it feel like*
*to let yourself believe this, just as an experiment?*

**2.** *Each day when you wake up, greet yourself with*
*"Good morning (your name)." And if you are really*
*brave try saying "Good morning, I love you (your name).*
*Good morning, I have compassion for you (your name)."*

*I invite you to try saying this in different tones of voice,*
*softly, loudly, whispering it, silently... See what feels*
*most authentic and what most resonates in your body.*

*Play with it. Add movement or physical touch*
*to the words. I found that putting my hand over my heart*
*when I greeted myself significantly increased*
*the felt sense of love and compassion.*

**3.** *Share your experience with one dear friend,*
*and invite them to do the practice with you.*
*Each morning you will say,*
*"Good morning, I love you (your name).*
*Good morning, I have compassion for you (your name)."*

*Then say to each other in turn,*
*"Good morning, I love you (your friend's name).*
*Good morning I have compassion for you (your friend's name)."*

# 8

KRISTIN NEFF, PhD, chose this quote:

**"**

Compulsive concern with 'I, me, and mine' isn't the same as loving ourselves... Loving ourselves points us to capacities of resilience, compassion, and understanding that are simply part of being alive.

**"**

*Sharon Salzberg,* The Force of Kindness, *2005*

## THEME – *Accessing Natural Self-Compassion*

I love this quote because it reminds us that self-compassion is actually a process of letting go. **When our hearts are open — when we allow ourselves to be touched by our own pain — we naturally respond with feelings of caring concern.** This isn't something we have to intentionally make happen. Rather, it is the very nature of the heart itself, a capacity merely to be uncovered rather than created anew. But what is it that's covering our hearts and preventing our love from flowing freely? The sense of a separate self.

When we see ourselves as distinct and cut off from others, we become obsessed with questions of who and what we are. Am I good or am I bad? Am I better than you or worse than you? Do I deserve compassion? Am I worthy of love?

When we recognize our shared and interconnected humanity, however, these concerns become irrelevant. **Love is experienced in any moment of true connection — with others,** with ourselves or with our moment-to-moment experience. Love is limitless because everything is connected, whether considered from the subatomic, cellular, psychological, social or global point of view. In order to know love, compassion and well-being, therefore, we only have to open our eyes to what's already here. **When we recognize our essential interconnectedness, we naturally find our resilient and boundless hearts.**

One way to access your natural self-compassion is to constantly remind yourself of your common humanity. When you find yourself lost in pain, self-criticism or feelings of unworthiness, try to remember that the human experience is imperfect – a reality we all share. Take a moment to consider how many countless others have had experiences so similar to your own. Rather than feeling isolated from others when you confront something in yourself or your life that you don't like, remember that nothing is wrong, abnormal or aberrant in imperfection. You are not alone. **By softening your sense of separate self in this way, your innate feelings of love and compassion will be able to emerge more freely.**

*One way to access your natural self-compassion
is to constantly remind yourself of your
common humanity. For the next week,
whenever you find yourself lost in pain,
self-criticism or feelings of unworthiness,
try to do two things:*

■

*Remember that the human experience is imperfect —
this is a reality we all share. Say something out loud
like "Imperfection is just part of life."*

■

*Take a moment to consider how many countless
others have had experiences so similar to your own.
Try to imagine all the diverse and varied ways
people have gone through just what
you're going through right now.*

■

*If you feel isolated from others when you confront
something in yourself or your life that you don't like,
try to remember that nothing is wrong, abnormal
or aberrant in imperfection. You are not alone.
By softening your sense of separate self in this way,
your innate feelings of love and compassion
will be able to emerge more freely.*

*Quotes № 9 to 15*

# Compassion Readiness

# 9

MICHAEL MEADE, DHL, chose this quote

" 

# In the beginner's mind there are many possibilities, in the expert's mind there are few.

,,

*Shunryu Suzuki*

## THEME – *Developing a Compassionate Beginner's Mind – Shoshin*

Becoming more compassionate at a meaningful level can result in a greater capacity for openness to both inner and outer experiences, as described in the Zen practice of *shoshin or beginner's mind*. Taking the attitude of a beginner makes us less subject to preconceived ideas and less restricted by preformed judgments. Being ready to begin anew diminishes automatic reactions based upon old patterns of behavior. Whether an event appears surprising, threatening or tragic, it can be experienced with a fresh mind.

As the quote from Zen teacher Suzuki suggests, the expert may have dogmatic certainty, but **the openness of the beginner is more likely to find the true nature of a situation. Expert comes from experience, yet no amount of experience can add up to wisdom. Wisdom requires a willingness to learn and even a capacity to be foolish in the right direction.** Shoshin begins where common experience and accepted procedures leave off. **It offers a particular kind of compassion, a wisdom practice based on a willingness to sit or walk or even dance at the edge where life remains open to many possibilities and as yet unseen potentials.**

Like most enduring words, *shoshin* has more than one meaning. The same word that designates the practice of *beginner's mind can also mean correct truth.* When used in that sense, it denotes "a genuine signature on a work of art" or refers "to an item or person that is genuine." Thus, the practice of beginner's mind also involves the sense of originality that makes art compelling, as well as the authenticity that makes a person unique and valuable. Here, there seems to be a surprising ground, an open area where Eastern philosophies can encounter and exchange with Western ideas.

## COMPASSION PRACTICE FOR THE WEEK

*Track the subtle ways that eternity tries to visit you, whether it be through silent meditation or ecstatic dance.* **Instead of being busy find more openings to timelessness. Find at least one moment of eternity in each day; refuse to go to sleep until you do so.**

*Choose a book of poems from a poet like Rumi, Hafiz or Rilke or an author of similar imagination and courage. Make sure the writer is capable of surprise like the Zen rascal Ikkyu who wrote:*

*"If you break open the cherry tree, Where are the flowers? But in the springtime, see how they bloom!"*

*You want to sit at the feet of the words and be there when the blooming happens. You want the randomly chosen words to carry you to where the beginnings endlessly blossom and your beginner's mind opens again like the timeless lotus on the ancient pond.*

## 10

RICHARD FIELDS, PhD, chose this quote:

**"**

# The essence of bravery is being without self-deception.

**"**

*Pema Chodron*

### THEME – *Overcoming Self-Deception (Delusion)*

Self-deception is the opposite of awareness.
*Denial is a way to avoid the fact that you might have a problem. It is a form of self-delusion. Practicing to not deceive ourselves, with eyes and heart open, invites awareness and self-discovery.*

Having worked for over thirty years in the addictions field, I am no stranger to recognizing the signs of denial.

A good way to remember "denial" is the acronym:

**D** – **Don't**

**E** – **Even**

**N** – **kNow**

**I** – **I**

**A** – **Am**

**L** – **Lying.**

We all have self-deceptions and delusions, and how humbling it is when we begin to awake from them. It is painful to see our own faults and mistakes. It's so much easier to choose delusion over awareness.

There are common delusions about who we are in the world, as compared with who we think we are. So you can see why Pema Chodron considers it a brave act to be without self-deception (delusion).

### COMPASSION PRACTICE FOR THE WEEK

*This week try to see things as they are. Ask yourself the question "Am I lying to myself?" periodically throughout your day. Ask further questions to clarify.*

*Try not to judge, but instead accept. Explore whether you might be hiding from some truth or fear that may be painful and cause suffering.*

## 11

RONALD D. SIEGEL, PsyD, chose this quote:

66

# What you resist, persists.

99

*Attributed to Carl Jung*

## THEME – *Awareness of What Arises*

Of all the mechanisms of the mind revealed through compassion practice, resistance may cause the most grief. It plays a central role in my own suffering and in most of the problems that prompt people to seek counseling.

Some examples are obvious: Who hasn't noticed that trying to fall asleep can cause sleepless nights, trying to stay calm can make us agitated and trying to maintain sexual arousal is the fastest way to lose it? And who doesn't know people who drink to feel better, only to wind up feeling worse; *or who constrict their lives out of fear, only to grow more fearful?*

Other examples are a bit more subtle: The pious person who eschews sexual feelings only to be plagued by them, the kind person who denies angry feelings only to have them emerge as mysterious bodily pains or passive-aggressive behavior, or the tough, masculine guy who feels compelled to attack split-off aspects of himself that he sees in more sensitive types.

**All of these maladies involve experiential avoidance — trying to make uncomfortable feelings, sensations or thoughts go away.**

**It's a strategy that almost all of us try, but it never works for long, and it usually backfires, for when we bury feelings, we bury them alive.**

Compassion practice offers an alternative. *By turning our attention toward whatever arises in consciousness, whether pleasurable or painful, and trying to open fully to our experience, we enable the mind to operate with greater ease.* We notice that no feeling, thought or sensation lasts indefinitely. We also stop accumulating disavowed, split-off feelings that cause anxiety by threatening to flood into consciousness the moment we slow down. **By opening ourselves up to pleasure and pain, we're not plagued by so many symptoms.**

Another benefit of embracing our experience is that it leads to compassion toward ourselves and others, for whatever pain or evil we see in other people we've already seen and accepted in our own heart and mind. The world is no longer populated by good and bad people, us and them, but only by struggling fellow beings.

## COMPASSION PRACTICE FOR THE WEEK

### *Embracing Experience*

*When we find ourselves wishing our mind would be other than it is, pushing away or distracting ourselves from something uncomfortable, we can simply ask,* **"What am I resisting here?"** *It often helps to close our eyes and bring attention to sensations in the body — to notice where there's tightness, constriction or perhaps the hint of an emotion. We can then breathe into these sensations and ask ourselves, "What might this be?" Sometimes an image or thought will come to mind that illuminates the resistance, letting us see what we're having difficulty accepting. True to the principal that "what we resist, persists," a gentle balance is needed, so we practice accepting our resistance as we begin to let it go.*

## 12

BILL MORGAN, PsyD, chose this quote:

> **We can never understand the nature of the mind through intense effort but only by relaxing, just as breaking a wild horse requires that one approach it gently and treat it kindly rather than running after it and trying to use force.**

*Kalu Rinpoche*

## THEME – *Compassion Involves Relaxation*

In the old days relaxation was considered to be unimportant in meditation practice, since it allegedly had nothing to do with the freedom we were seeking in the practice of meditation. Plop down and pay attention was the basic format for practice. **Now I see relaxation as central and fundamental, the ground for both compassion and insight. How can compassion arise in a tense body and constricted breath?**

Though we understand this conceptually, seldom does relaxation get the attention it deserves in meditation practice. We are so tense in this culture. Relaxing at the beginning of a meditation session is in itself a profound act of self-care. So too does self-compassion require the relaxing of the breath, mind, and body.

## COMPASSION PRACTICE FOR THE WEEK

### *Compassionate Relaxation in Three Parts:*

### *1. Shaking It Loose*

*Helping the body to relax is step one. There are a number of ways to do this. These days there is more exposure to yoga, tai chi, qigong. It doesn't have to be fancy. Jack LaLanne jumping jacks are still available. I used to watch Romper Room when I was 4 or 5, and I still remember joining in this exercise:*

> *Bend and stretch,*
> *Reach for the stars,*
> *Here comes Jupiter,*
> *There goes Mars.*

*That works for me as well as any of the imported approaches. Pretending you are an animal, getting down on the floor and crawling around for a couple of minutes and making the appropriate animal sounds, can also do the trick. Shake out the arms and legs. Do a few neck rolls. The form doesn't matter. What does matter is getting the body a bit more loose and pliable. If you can add a playful dimension right at the start, that's an added bonus.*

### *2. Taking Your Seat*

*I am not an advocate of straight-as-a-board posture. Nothing else in nature is that straight. You want to be reasonably upright, but also at ease. As you are settling into your posture, try raising and lowering the shoulders, making fists for a few seconds, or opening the mouth wide for a moment or two. These are places where tension is commonly carried. I often scrunch up my face for a few seconds, which brings a childlike sensibility into the moment, just before closing the eyes.*

### 3. Settling the Breath

*Now close the eyes, and imagine letting the weight of the body settle
more deeply, giving in to the downward pull of gravity.*

*Take two or three deeper than usual breaths. As you exhale, imagine
that the tension and stress are leaving the body, knots of tension
melting as the energy moves down through you.*

*Allow the breath to establish a smooth, easy rhythm as the body
continues to relax and the energy moves down and down, as if you
were safely secured in a diving bell which was lowering
you beneath the waves, beneath the turbulent thoughts and
feelings on the surface of the mind, to a quieter and deeper place.*

*You are watching over this settling process in a kindly, caring way,
keeping the breath soft. You can look up at the surface and see
the thoughts and feelings up above, but they do not disturb you.*

*As you become more relaxed, you may begin to notice a pleasant,
contented feeling begin to arise. Slowly this feeling begins
to spread, to radiate throughout the body and mind,
and you are watching over this. Enjoy it.*

*Now, letting go of the imagery, remain sitting and
breathing in this atmosphere of comfort and ease.*

■

*Feel free to explore your own imagery. I have found the downward
flow of energy to be particularly effective in evoking relaxation.*

■

*Watching over the process keeps the mind engaged in a mindful posture.
You don't want to get lost in the imagery or in drifting; knowing
what is happening as it is happening is a hallmark of mindfulness.*

■

*The purpose of visualizing is to evoke a particular affect –
in this case relaxation and ease. As the affect becomes stable
you can gradually let go of the "training wheels" of imagery*

# 13

**66**

My goal isn't to be thin.
My goal is for my body to be
the weight it can hold – to be strong
and healthy and fit, to be itself.
My goal is to learn to embrace
this body and to be grateful
every day for what it has given me.

**99**

*Oprah Winfrey*

## THEME – *Compassion for Our Body:*
## *"Being Healthy – That Always Looks Good"*

Self-compassion is essential to help us through the epic struggle to accept our bodies. **We often tear ourselves to shreds with self-criticism when we don't look the way we think we're supposed to – especially women.** We stare at the super-thin, aerobicized models on the covers of magazines and, not surprisingly, don't feel we measure up. Even the cover girls don't feel they measure up, since most images are digitally enhanced. Given the value placed on beauty in our society, it's not surprising that perceived attractiveness is one of the most important areas in which women invest their sense of self-worth. This is a problem, given research indicating that four out of five American women are dissatisfied with the way they look and that over half are on a diet at any one time. Almost 50% of all girls between first and third grade say they want to be thinner and, by age 18, fully 80% of girls report that they have dieted at some point in their life.

How can we end the suffering caused by our endless criticism of our bodies? By opening our hearts and stopping the internal war. With self-compassion, we don't need to be perfect in order to feel good about ourselves. We can drop the obsessive fixation with being thin enough or pretty enough and accept ourselves as we are; even revel in who we are. **Being comfortable in our own skin allows us to focus on what's really important: being healthy – and that always looks good.**

## COMPASSION PRACTICE FOR THE WEEK – BODY SCAN

### *Body-Acceptance Meditation*

*This exercise takes about 25 minutes. It's a variation of the meditation commonly known as "the body scan." It's best to lie down on a bed or the floor in what's known as the "corpse pose" in yoga. First, place your hands on your heart as a reminder to be kind to yourself. Feel the warmth of your hands and take three deep, relaxing breaths. Then place your arms by your side again.*

*Slowly and systematically scan your attention throughout your body. You can go in any order you choose, but a common order is as follows: Start by becoming aware of your right foot, then move your awareness up to your right calf, right thigh, then over to your left foot, left calf, left thigh, to your buttocks, lower back, upper back, pelvic area, stomach, chest, right shoulder, right upper arm, right lower arm, right hand, left shoulder, left upper arm, left lower arm, left hand, neck, face, back of head, top of head.*

As you scan, try to bring a sense of gratitude and appreciation to the particular body part you're noticing. For instance, being thankful to your feet for allowing you to walk, your hands for allowing you to pet your dog, your stomach for digesting your food, your neck for holding up your head, etc.

While you're scanning also notice if any negative judgments are coming up around that body part, for instance that your thighs are too big, arms too weak, stomach too flabby, etc. Whenever these judgments arise, give yourself compassion for the difficulty of being an imperfect human. Everyone has aspects of their body they're unhappy with; it is part of the shared human experience. Try to be kind, supportive, and understanding towards yourself as you confront the suffering caused by our continual dissatisfaction with our bodies.

The main idea of this meditation is that as you become aware of each body part, you cultivate both appreciation for how it helps you and also compassion for any negative judgments about it.

When you have scanned your entire body, put your hands on your heart again and expand your awareness to your whole body, giving it a shower of affection and gratitude. Then hold your entire body in compassionate awareness. Can you – just for this moment – accept yourself and your body exactly as you are? Love yourself exactly as you are?

Then gently open your eyes.

## 14

ELISHA GOLDSTEIN, PhD, chose this quote:

**"**

# Wherever you are, that is the entry point.

**"**

*Kabir, 15th-century Indian poet*

## THEME – *Being In "The Here and Now"*

These are the last four lines of the Diamond Sutra. Aren't they beautiful?

"Who can hang onto a star or a bubble? Like an orchid in your meditation area, these lines suggest that impermanence is not about absence, or even loss, but instead about the beauty implicit in ephemeral things – which, luckily enough, is everything."

*Compassion, when fully engaged, allows us to inhabit the here and now, where stars emerge, bubbles burst and flashes of lightning come and go.* None of these things last, nor do we. Trying to make it not so, hanging on to moments beyond their shelf lives — in fact, turning them into phantoms or dreams — leads to a special type of suffering. When I was a kid, this would happen when I would catch a butterfly, but then inadvertently kill it by "keeping" it in a jar. I loved it! Why did it die?

As an adult, I hang on to myself and loved ones, my personal history, my iPhone and really good take-out. And the occasional Chardonnay. And, OK, other stuff too. There's nothing intrinsically wrong with that, except that it means I have a lot to lose, and losing brings pain. And it can mutate into ongoing suffering when its source is an attachment to how things are supposed to be, rather than an acceptance of how they really are. **The Diamond Sutra counsels us to let the butterfly go, to let ourselves love and need, but to do so without a tight grasp or any expectations of durability.**

This is the gift of compassion. The here and now, when allowed to be so, contains reality and beauty. The orchid is beautiful when blooming, beautiful when dropping its petals, beautiful when a naked stem and beautiful when compost. **It's only when we try to keep it in full flower that we kill it in our minds.** Nothing wrong with that, either, I guess. Except that we miss a lot, and feel bad when we don't have to.

## COMPASSION PRACTICE FOR THE WEEK

*The world around us is an ongoing meditation on arising and falling away, on the impermanence of all things. We suffer when we try to keep this natural cycle from unfolding, as it inevitably will.*

*This week, see if you can notice the constant coming and going, shifting and changing, of things around you without trying to evaluate or alter them. The sound of a car alarm, a homeless guy yelling at you, the smell of coffee, someone crying, a bird flitting by, a worry. Compassion in this context means that you "just" experience these things, letting them happen without judging them, without making them stay or go. Is it possible to experience this flash of lightning, that butterfly, without jarring them up? Sometimes when this happens, joy emerges from circumstances that otherwise might go unappreciated. This meditation needs no cushion. It can happen anywhere, at any time.*

# 15

DANIEL J. SIEGEL, MD, chose this quote:

**❝**

# You must be the change you wish to see in the world.

**❞**

*Mahatma Gandhi*

## THEME – *Being the Change:*
## *Awareness of Awareness & Attention to Intention*

This often-cited quotation is not usually offered as an example of compassion, but for me it serves as a powerful and succinct reminder of the essence of what compassion means. Compassion is certainly a state of awareness involving a set of qualities in the present moment in which we focus attention without being swept up by prejudgments. Some also place being kind and compassionate to ourselves as a part of the texture of this mindful state. *Compassion and compassion practice are also a set of traits described as a way of being that is imbued with being awake to what is happening as it is happening, of having emotional equanimity, of being able to sense the inner nature of our mental lives.*

In both compassion states and compassionate traits, there is a way of being that we can strive for that brings internal balance and interpersonal connection. *The words from Mahatma Gandhi remind us that change begins with ourselves.* If we want to see kindness and compassion in the world, we must begin with kindness and compassion within ourselves. **If we want others to have clarity of focus, to be present for life as it unfolds, to be awake to the wondrous mysteries of this time we call our lives, then we must begin to cultivate these very qualities ourselves.**

## COMPASSION PRACTICE FOR THE WEEK

*Within these words, too, we see the two powerful aspects of all mindful awareness practices:*

## *"Awareness of awareness,*
## *and*
## *attention to intention."*

*To be the change we wish to see in the world, we need to be aware of our awareness, to hold within this place of knowing our own unfolding sense of being awake. The notion of being the change "you wish to see in the world" also requires that we hold our own intention in the front of our minds — that we pay attention to our intention. In these many ways, Gandhi was offering to us a powerful sentiment at the heart of what it means to be compassionate. Taken into our hearts and heads, our minds can bring compassion into the world from the inside out. Not bad for a dozen words!*

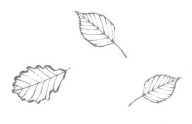

*Quotes № 16 to 20*

# Opening Your Compassionate Heart

QUOTE #16 – Halifax
*Compassion is a Necessity*

QUOTE #17 – Brach
*Tonglen: Awakening the Heart of Compassion
by Unlocking the Armor of Our Heart*

QUOTE #18 – Kornfield
*Compassion & the Heart*

QUOTE #19 – Lokos
*The Compassionate Heart Center*

QUOTE #20 - Schwartz
*The Secret Beauty of the Heart*

# 16

ROSHI JOAN HALIFAX, PhD, chose this quote:

66

# Love and compassion are necessities, not luxuries. Without them humanity cannot survive.

99

*His Holiness the Dalai Lama*

## THEME – *Compassion is a Necessity*

Compassion is a precious necessity for all of us. **We all need to cultivate compassion in our lives. It is one of our most treasured social assets and nourishes the human heart,** plus it is good for others. What would our world be without compassion? How could we live without compassion? What would our world be with more compassion? Compassion in our schools, in our government, in our hospitals, in our media? Why don't we vote based on compassion? Why don't we train our kids in compassion? **I want to live in a world where compassion is valued, don't you?**

## COMPASSION PRACTICE FOR THE WEEK

*First find a quiet moment, a quiet space. Let your heart and mind settle. Then recall someone to whom you feel especially close, someone whom you deeply wish to be free of suffering, whether the suffering is physical, social, mental, or spiritual.*

*As you experience how this might feel, breathe deeply into your belly and track whatever you are sensing physically.*

*Recall that person's humanness and good qualities, as well as the suffering that he or she has been through or is going through.*

*Now internally repeat simple phrases of compassion toward the person you have visualized. With your breath, silently say to him or her:*

**May you be free from this suffering.**
**May you be safe.**
**May you find peace.**

*Continue to visualize this person as you breathe and silently say to him or her:*

**May you be free from this suffering.**
**May you be safe.**
**May you find peace.**

*And for a final time, visualizing your friend or relative silently and sincerely say to him or her:*

**May you be free from this suffering.**
**May you be safe.**
**May you find peace.**

*Let your wish for this one person help strengthen your aspiration to help others.*

## 17

TARA BRACH, PhD, chose this quote:

❝

# Could a greater miracle take place than for us to look through each other's eyes for an instant?

❞

*Henry David Thoreau*, Walden, *1854, in*
The Writings of Henry David Thoreau, *vol. 2, 1906, p. 11*

## THEME – Tonglen: *Awakening the Heart of Compassion by Unlocking the Armor of Our Heart*

**The capacity for compassion is hardwired into our brain and body.** Just as we are rigged to perceive differences, to feel separate, and to react with aversion, we are also designed to feel a connection with our fellow humans. **Specialized "mirror neurons" attune us to another person's state** – to their emotions and the intentions behind their movements – and recreate that state in our own brain. Our experience of them is not just a projection based on visible expressions like grimaces, narrowed eyes, or furrowed brows. Because of mirror neurons, and other structures in the prefrontal cortex that make up our compassion circuitry, we can actually "feel with" them.

**Yet these compassion circuits are easily blocked when we're stressed and out of touch with our emotions and bodies.** They can also become blocked when we're experiencing unexamined reactivity to the people in our life. Research shows that the less we identify with someone – the less they seem real to us – the less the mirror neuron system gets activated.

The good news is that we can unblock and activate our compassion networks. When we mindfully recognize that another is hurt or afraid, we naturally feel the tenderness of compassion. That tenderness blossoms fully as we find ways to express our care. This alchemy of letting ourselves be touched by another's pain and of responding with love is the essence of Buddhist compassion practices.

One such meditation, the Tibetan practice of *tonglen*, directly awakens our capacity for seeing through another's eyes and offering care. **The starting place in *tonglen* is an intentional relaxing of the armoring around our heart.** Each of us has been wounded, and in reaction, has erected defenses to protect ourselves from experiencing further harm. We don't want to be vulnerable or available to pain. Yet before we can be tenderhearted, we have to be tender. As poet Mark Nepo writes:

**"Our challenge each day is not to get dressed to face the world, but to unglove ourselves so that the doorknob feels cold, and the car handle feels wet, and the kiss goodbye feels like the lips of another being, soft and unrepeatable."**

**Compassion – for ourselves, each other, and all living beings – is an innate part of our evolutionary potential.** While we have strong conditioning to close down, we also aspire to awaken our hearts and realize our belonging to each other. This longing is the compass of our heart; it is our guide to happiness, freedom, and the healing of our world.

Tonglen: *Awakening the Heart of Compassion*

*Sit in a way that allows you to be relaxed and alert. Let go of any habitual tension and allow your body and mind to settle.*

*The traditional practice of* tonglen *begins by taking a moment to sense the stillness or openness that is already here. This is considered a flash of remembrance, a reconnecting with our awakened heart and mind.*

*Now bring your attention to the natural rhythm and quality of your breath. As the breath flows in, allow your cells to receive this life energy. With each in breath, open with total receptivity, like a balloon gently expanding with air. Be aware of the experience of no resistance, of allowing yourself to be touched by the sensations of the breath.*

*With the out- breath, notice the sensations of letting go and releasing into the space that surrounds you. Imagine your total body and consciousness flowing outward with the breath and mingling with the vastness of space. Breathe out into relaxation, ease, and spaciousness.*

*Continue meditating on the essence of receiving, being touched with the in- breath, and letting go into openness with the out- breath.*

*Now invite into your awareness someone you know personally who is suffering, someone you want to help. Imagine yourself in this person's circumstances, experiencing this person's fear or hurt or loss. What is it like to look at the world through these eyes? Live inside this particular body? Feel with this heart? What is the most vulnerable, painful part of this person's experience? What does he or she most need?*

*Now breathing in, invite all this pain into your heart, allowing yourself to feel it fully. Breathe in, taking the pain into yourself, so that the other person will have relief.*

*And as you breathe out, respond to his or her needs by sending out relaxation, space, love, or whatever will bring ease and happiness.*

*Sometimes as you breathe in, you will meet your own resistance to pain. If this happens, shift the focus and breathe for yourself and countless others just like you who are feeling this same frustration, anger, revulsion, or fear. Then as you breathe out, offer whatever helps you and others like you find space and relief.*

*As your resistance softens, return to breathing for the person*
*you intend to help. As you inhale and let the person's pain touch you,*
*feel how he or she is held in your heart. And as you exhale, send whatever*
*prayer or expression of care feels most sincere or most needed.*

*Now, enlarge the taking in and sending out to include all those who are in*
*the same situation, experiencing the same suffering. If the person you want to*
*help is grieving a loss, breathe in and out for all those who are experiencing*
*the pain of loss. If this person feels like a failure, breathe in and out for all*
*who feel like failures. Sense, as you breathe in, the unconditional willingness,*
*tenderness, and receptivity of your heart; and as you breathe out, the vastness*
*of loving awareness that is here, holding this world.*

*Continue breathing, opening to the universal experience of this suffering*
*and letting go into spaciousness with prayer. As your heart opens to the*
*enormity of suffering, you become that openness. As you offer your tenderness,*
*your awareness becomes suffused with compassion.*

*Flexibility in using the breath: If at any point you find the breathing*
*instructions interfere with the actual experience of taking in suffering and*
*sending out ease and love, adjust to however it most serves the meditation.*
*For instance, you might find you need to focus on just the in- breath or just the*
*out- breath for several cycles to more fully contact experience, or to let go.*
*Or you might find that it is easier not to focus on the breath at all.*

*Throughout your day: You can do an abbreviated version of tonglen whenever*
*you encounter suffering. If someone you meet is having a hard time, pause.*
*For several breaths, silently breathe in his or her pain and breathe out relief.*
*If you feel yourself resisting, turned off, or afraid of the pain, do tonglen for*
*yourself and all those like you who are having difficulty opening to pain.*

**No matter what comes up, it is an opportunity for practicing compassion.**
**Rather than ignoring pain or judging ourselves, we can train ourselves**
**to open into our full potential to love.**

*Note: Tonglen may be inappropriate if you are struggling with trauma-*
*related fear, unrelenting depression, or severe psychological imbalance.*
*Tonglen may then cause emotional flooding or a sense of being stuck.*
*In these situations, seek guidance from a spiritual teacher, therapist,*
*or trusted guide in finding what best helps you move toward healing.*

## 18

JACK KORNFIELD, PhD, chose this quote:

# Oh nobly born, remember your own loving heart. Trust it, honor it, follow it. It will bring you peace.

*The Buddha*

## THEME – *Compassion & the Heart*

**The human heart has the extraordinary capacity to transform the sorrows of life into a great stream of compassion.** Compassion proclaims the power of the tender and merciful heart in the face of the suffering of the world. It arises whenever we allow our heart to be touched by the pain and need of another.

## COMPASSION PRACTICE FOR THE WEEK

*To cultivate compassion, let yourself sit in a centered and quiet way. Breathe softly and feel your body, your heartbeat, and the life within you. Feel how you treasure your own life, how you guard yourself in the face of your sorrow.*

*After some time, bring to mind someone close to you whom you dearly love. Picture them and feel your natural caring for them. Notice how you hold them in your heart.*

*Then let yourself be aware of their sorrows, their measure of suffering in life. Feel how your heart opens to wish them well; to extend comfort to them; to share in their pain and meet them with compassion.*

*To open your heart still further, begin reciting the phrases:*
*"May you be held in compassion.*
*May your pain and sorrows be eased.*
*May you be at peace."*

*Continue reciting the phrases while you are holding them in your heart.*

*After you feel your deep caring for this person close to you, turn the same compassionate heart toward yourself.*

*Place your hands over your own heart, while you recite.*
*"May I be held in compassion,*
*May my pain and sorrow be eased.*
*May I be at peace."*

*Now, one person at a time, extend your compassion to others you know. Picture loved ones, one after another. Hold the image of each in your heart, be aware of their difficulties and wish them well, as you recite:*
*"May you be held in compassion.*
*May your pain and sorrow be eased.*
*May you be at peace."*

*Now you can open your compassion further to the suffering of your friends, to your neighbors, your community, to all who suffer, to difficult people, to your enemies, and finally to the brotherhood and sisterhood of all beings.*

## 19

ALLAN LOKOS chose this quote:

##

The door to the human
heart can be opened only
from the inside.

*Spanish Proverb*

# THEME – *The Compassionate Heart Center*

Even the greatest of poets cannot describe the depth of compassion and love that the human heart can experience. **In spiritual practice, we refer to the "heart center" rather than the heart as an organ.** It can be an indicator of what is going on within us. We're so inundated with "get out there and do it" messages that the energy spent just being with another person can appear to be doing nothing at all. Yet, connecting heart to heart is anything *but* doing nothing. Being in touch with our heart center and making genuine heart-to-heart contact with another requires energy and attentiveness. How do we start? What can we do in our busy lives to be more in touch with our own heart center? We could start by stopping – stopping to take a moment in stillness. We could enjoy a long gentle in-breath and a long outward sigh. (How about right now?) We could lighten up – even a little bit can help. **A heart can become heavy both spiritually and physiologically, especially when its companion is a relentless mind.** We could walk on the earth (even if it's paved over with concrete), smell a flower, sing a song, dance with a friend, and offer a smile to that person in the mirror.

Our greatest happiness comes from the experience of love and compassion. The more we genuinely care about others, the greater our own happiness and inner peace. So, loving others is the greatest gift we can give ourselves. It's almost a contradiction – altruism that rewards one's self. For each of us, there are those we find easier to love and those we find more challenging. But the practice of being a loving, compassionate person allows no boundaries; no one can be excluded. Those who push our buttons – who appear rude, arrogant, greedy – these are the very people with whom we can refine our practice. No matter how different the look, behavior, customs, or costumes, there is no significant difference among people. A loving, compassionate person recognizes that our basic natures are the same. We all want to be happy and we all want to be loved.

*Each day, offer thoughts of loving kindness to
yourself and to all beings.*

*Think gently to yourself:
May all beings be safe.
May all beings be happy.
May all beings be healthy.
May all beings live with ease.
May all beings live in peace.
May my life be of benefit to all beings.
To "live with ease" refers to dealing with our everyday activities –
home life, the workplace, the kids, traffic, and so forth –
free from stress and turmoil.
If you are going through a difficult period,
or if it just feels right, it's fine to focus
primarily on yourself: May I be safe, may I be happy, etc.*

*If you know of someone who is going through a
particularly difficult time, you might want to focus
primarily on him or her. Envision them and think:
May you be safe, may you be happy, etc. It's nice to end by
offering* metta *to all beings: May all beings be safe, etc.
Feel free to alter the wording so that it feels right for you.
Offer the thoughts at a pace that enables you to
maintain concentration from one sentence to the next.*

RICHARD C. SCHWARTZ, PhD, chose this quote:

"

Then it was as if I suddenly saw the secret beauty of their hearts, the depth of their hearts where neither sin nor desire nor self-knowledge can reach, the core of their reality, the person that each one is in the eyes of the Divine. If only they could all see themselves as they really are. If only we could see each other that way all the time. There would be no more war, no more hatred, no more greed... I suppose the big problem would be that we would fall down and worship each other.

"

*Thomas Merton*

# THEME – *The Secret Beauty of The Heart*

If you have had an experience like the one Merton describes, it is unforgettable, but also fleeting. **There are protective parts of all of us that maintain the optical delusion of separateness.** They limit our ability to see the divine beauty in others, and, relatedly, keep our circle of compassion small so we are not overwhelmed by the pain in the world and don't spend all our time trying to change it.

**Fortunately, however, there is a place within us where we know we are connected to the sacred in each other and, consequently, from that place we have an enormous circle of compassion.** I call this inner essence the Self and find that it is just behind the walls erected by our inner protectors. This means that we don't have to meditate twenty years before we can attain it. Instead this calm, compassionate Self will emerge spontaneously once the parts of us that occlude it trust that it is safe to relax and open space inside.

## COMPASSION PRACTICE FOR THE WEEK

*No matter how hard we work to be openhearted we all have parts of us (sometimes unconscious) that give us negative or fearful thoughts and emotions regarding a person we consider different or dangerous.*

*Think of such a person in your life that you fear or disdain, or a group of people that, at some level, you fear or disdain, and then imagine a single person from that group. Notice how you feel toward this person as you consider him or her. Now, pretend that you have x-ray vision and can see inside that person. As you look inside, notice that the protective parts of that person that scare you or that you don't like are protecting their hurt and vulnerable parts.*

*Then notice that, deep within them, behind both the protection and vulnerability, is a radiant, pulsating light. Stay focused on that light until you start to feel it in yourself, beneath your own protective parts. Look again at the person and see how you feel toward him or her now.*

# Compassion & Connection

## 21

CHRIS GERMER, PhD, chose this quote:

> Admit something:
> Everyone you see, you say to them,
> 'Love me.' Of course you do not do this
> out loud, otherwise someone would
> call the cops. Still, though, think about
> this, this great pull in us to connect.
> Why not become the one who lives
> with a full moon in each eye that is
> always saying, with that sweet moon
> language, what every other eye in this
> world is dying to hear?

*Hafiz,* With That Moon Language, in
The Gift: Poems by Hafiz, the great Sufi Master,
*D. Ladinsky, trans., 1999*

## THEME – *The Desire & Drive to Be Loved & to Love*

These words come to us from the 14th century, but they could easily have been written today. **The pull to connect is a deep urge or drive within all human beings**, as it is in most mammals that have learned to survive by connecting with one another.

If newborn babies could speak, their first words might sound a lot like "Love me!" Fortunately, babies are good at getting adults to love them and whatever they need naturally follows.

**Do we ever stop saying, "Love me" just because our bodies have aged? I doubt it. Like children, we look for signs of warmth and friendliness in the eyes of almost everyone we meet and we feel subtly wounded if a whole day passes without receiving any affection.** A host of good feelings arise when we feel loved, such as joy, gratitude, generosity, and hope. Similarly, the pain of disconnection from others is associated with negative emotions such as anger, fear, and shame.

Curiously, we tend to forget the wise words of Hafiz and live our lives as if it doesn't matter whether we're loved, spending much of our lives in pursuit of material possessions and using people to achieve our personal goals rather than valuing warmth and connection. Perhaps the pain of disconnection has made us stop caring. But what would happen if we woke up every morning consciously aware that, like all human beings, we wish to be loved? The root of compassion is intimate contact with suffering. How about the universal hunger to be seen, heard, touched, and known? When our hearts are open to this yearning, we seem to discover the same in others and respond in kind.

The opposite reaction is sadly familiar. When we forget that everyone wishes to be loved and when the pain of disconnection arrives at our door, our feelings become hard, often with anger and resentment. But **when we peel back the onion of anger, we find softer emotions lying underneath, such as fear, loneliness, or confusion.** And still deeper, we discover the unmet need to be loved and connected. Lingering in awareness with this underlying need can protect us from a lot of unnecessary anguish.

To love and be loved is part of your deepest nature and is more essential than whatever or whoever you think you are.

**When we see how this "great pull in us to connect" motivates much of what we think and do, then the mind becomes quiet, the heart opens, and we begin to see others with new, more compassionate eyes.**

## COMPASSION PRACTICE FOR THE WEEK

*Before you get out of bed in the morning, put your hands over your heart and remind yourself, "I, and all beings, wish to be loved."*

## 22

STAN TATKIN, PsyD, MFT, chose this quote:

66

# Compassion automatically invites you to relate with people because you no longer regard people as a drain on your energy.

99

*Chögyam Trungpa*

## THEME – *Compassion: An Energy State*

Buddhist meditation master Chögyam Trungpa (1939-1987) spells out a benefit of compassion that I think also provides an important clue about how to cultivate it. **He refers to compassion as an energized state in which we naturally draw closer to others.** In psychological terms, we might say our ability **to be compassionate is inextricably tied to our perceived sense of security – both within ourselves and in our relationships.** Conversely, underlying insecurities can make it more difficult to feel compassion and give freely to others.

I suggest we begin by paying attention simply to how we feel around others. How comfortable are we? How easily do we feel drained or fatigued? How secure are we within ourselves?

When I work with couples in therapy, we ask these questions in the context of each partner's relationship style. While some individuals are fundamentally secure, others remain distant from their partner or harbor ambivalence. During our work, partners build their ability to keep each other secure and safe so they can readily repair any hurts, soothe as well as energize each other, and generally love more fully. In the process, they learn to give without fear and to stop seeing the other as a drain on their energy.

**What you may not realize is that your security and happiness depend to a large extent on your capacity to focus more on what you can give others than on what they can give you.** When you are in touch with your compassion as a giver – and that includes the ability to give compassion and to take care of yourself – you naturally feel energized around others.

Taking to heart the Rinpoche's words, you can move toward a more compassionate stance. Yes, compassion will invite you into more loving and fruitful relationships, but why wait for that invitation when you can take the first step right now?

## COMPASSION PRACTICE FOR THE WEEK

*You can practice the following whenever you spend time around another person.*

**1.** *Notice your comfort level: are you relaxed or tense, energized or drained? Don't try to change your feeling; just notice it.*

**2.** *Now consciously shift into the role of giver. This can be subtle – you don't have to say anything or give anything away – just view yourself as a giver. If you were already in that role, fine; just confirm it to yourself.*

**3.** *As you stay in the giver role, notice how you feel and act. Notice your energy level. Notice the state of your heart. Notice how the other person relates to you.*

*As you do this practice over time, see if you detect an increase in your sense of security, in your closeness with others, in your capacity for compassion.*

# 23

SHAUNA L. SHAPIRO, PhD, chose this quote:

**"**

# The fundamental delusion of humanity is to suppose that I am here and you are out there.

**"**

*Yasutani Hakuun Roshi (1885-1973)*

## THEME – *Interconnectedness*

**Compassion is our birthright. It is the natural response of a wise and open heart.** When our minds are clear and we are able to see the truth of our interconnectedness, the only appropriate response is one of helping compassion. For example, let's say that the left hand has a splinter in it. The right hand would naturally pull out the splinter, right? The left hand wouldn't say to the right hand, "Oh, thank you so much! You're so compassionate and generous!" The right hand removing the splinter is simply the appropriate response – it's just what the right hand does, because the two hands are part of the same body.

The more we practice compassionate awareness, the more we begin to see that we are all part of the same body – that "I," as the right hand, actually feel "you", the left hand's pain, and I naturally want to help. Compassion cultivates this interconnectedness and clear seeing, which leads to greater compassion and understanding of the mysterious web in which we all are woven. No one and no thing are separate. As Chief Seattle reminds us, "Humankind has not woven the web of life. We are but one thread within it. Whatever we do to the web, we do to ourselves. All things are bound together. All things connect."

**And so we begin to see that compassion isn't about being "good" or being "nice." Compassion is about seeing clearly and simply doing the only thing that makes sense.** If I have a splinter in one hand, the other hand takes it out. If I see a person or a nation suffering, my wisdom and compassion catalyze the natural human response to help alleviate this suffering. The Dalai Lama states that "the suffering of one person or one nation is the suffering of humanity. That the happiness of one person or nation is the happiness of humanity." Our compassion is not for someone else, that poor person over there separate from me. Compassion is felt for all of us because we are all in this together.

## COMPASSION PRACTICE FOR THE WEEK

*Sit quietly and comfortably, connecting gently with
the body and the breath. Invite in an intention
to see clearly the interconnectedness of all things.
Feel the wholesomeness of your intention and your
dedication to cultivate greater wisdom and compassion.
Let this intention nourish and motivate you.*

*Behold each other silently and relax your body.
Allow the breath to be natural. Notice how it feels to
be in the presence of another, to offer your full awareness.
Recognize that he or she is unique, different from
anyone else. Stay connected with your own body,
keeping 70% of you attention here, even as you*

# 24

ELISHA GOLDSTEIN, PhD, chose this quote:

**"**

# The biggest disease today is not leprosy or tuberculosis but rather the feeling of not belonging.

**"**

*Mother Teresa*

### THEME – *Making Connection & Belonging*

Mother Teresa saw too many people who were ostracized by society; she knew better than most the pain of not belonging. That pain lives in our culture.

One of the aims of the national research study I conducted in 2005 was to distill down the essence of feeling well. I discovered that the word people used more than any other to describe their experience of well-being was "connection."

**As human beings, we are wired toward connection. In order to feel healthy, we need to feel a sense of community, a sense that we belong and are not alone.** The problem is our culture makes it very difficult to belong from the start.

From the time when we are young, we are sent the message that we need to look a certain way or act a certain way in order to "fit in." We try to conform because, in our culture, we often don't accept those who are different. *In fact, history shows us that we fear those people who are different and often are quick to judge, isolate and even oppress them.*

So imagine that if belonging is so important to our health and well-being and we are a culture that is quick to cast out those who are different, it is easy for a deep-seeded fear to be planted in each of us from a very young age that perhaps we won't belong and that this would be intolerable. When we perceive that we don't belong, we look for ways to escape this intolerable feeling. These attempts to escape might include falling into a numb, depressed state; becoming anxious; or resorting to drugs, alcohol or other addictive behaviors.

Just think for a second: was there ever a time you didn't feel like you belonged or felt ostracized? What was your experience? What were you thinking and feeling?

*We thrive when we feel connection.*

**Psychologist Dr. Gary Schwartz has a handy model that says, "Awareness leads to connection which leads to balance; unawareness leads to disconnection, which leads to imbalance."** In other words, when we begin to cultivate an awareness of our thoughts, feelings and emotions, we become connected to them, which helps us become more balanced. When we are unaware of them or on auto-pilot, we are disconnected from them, and it is much more likely that they will take us over in fits of anxiety, anger or depression.

So connection can begin with us. We can begin by bringing compassionate awareness to our thoughts, feelings and/or emotions. Even just a few minutes of non-judgmental awareness of our feelings in any moment can be a moment of connection, balance and healing.

## COMPASSION PRACTICE FOR THE WEEK

*If you're feeling sadness, notice that sadness and bring a kind attention to where you feel that in the body, exploring it with a sense of curiosity and even imagining yourself holding this pain in your arms like you would imagine the archetypal nurturing mother figure doing (even though most of us did not have this, we might be able to imagine it). Just do this for a few minutes at a time and see what happens.*

*Always thank yourself for taking the time to do this. Time is precious and so giving time toward this is a gift, and that is why we try and send gratitude inwards.*

## 25

RICHARD FIELDS, PhD, chose this quote:

When you plant lettuce, if it does not grow well, you don't blame the lettuce. You look into the reasons it is not doing well. It may need fertilizer, or more water, or less sun. You never blame the lettuce. Yet if we have problems with our friends or our family, we blame the other person. But if we know how to take care of them, they will grow well, like lettuce. Blaming has no positive effect at all, nor does trying to persuade using reason and arguments... No blame, no reasoning, no argument, just understanding. If you understand, and you show that you understand, you can love, and the situation will change.

*Thich Nhat Hanh,* Peace Is Every Step, *1991, p. 78*

## THEME – *Understanding without Judgment*

**This quote clearly drives home the benefits of compassion and understanding and the negative impact of judging, lecturing, and directing. Listening without judgment, with attention, attunement, empathy, and sensitivity is preferred to persuading using reason and arguments.**

For example, a number of years ago, a young man, Brian, was referred to me for counseling. His parents were concerned that their son had dropped out of college to pursue a career as a member of a band.

I met with Brian individually for only one session and was impressed with his good looks, his affable but quiet personality, and his intelligence and overall smarts. He explained that the band was on the verge of signing a record deal, but it fell through at the last minute. He had not dropped out of school, but decided not to go back after the semester was over. He explained that he needed to spend all of his time and energy pursuing a new record contract and felt he had to put in 120% effort, without the distraction of schoolwork. He was young, 25 years old, and felt he had time for college.

Unfortunately, I had heard this story all too frequently without any positive outcomes, and made the judgment that he was wasting his time. I recommended that perhaps Brian take one course to just keep himself connected with college, a suggestion which he rejected outright.

A few years later I was in my counseling office and took a quick look at a new magazine that was just delivered. On the front cover of *Time* magazine there was a full-page picture of Brian and his fellow band members. I am so glad he never followed my advice.

### COMPASSION PRACTICE FOR THE WEEK

*When you sense that someone close to you might be ready, just sit with them; maybe ask a few questions about what might be going on in their life. Listen to them with understanding and compassion, no judgment, no problem solving, no reasoning – just acceptance.*

*Try this with family, friends, even new acquaintances, and see an improvement in compassion and connection.*

## 26

RONALD D. SIEGEL, PsyD, chose this quote:

66

# Love Thy Neighbor as Thyself is more than a commandment – it's a law of nature.

99

*A Patient*

## THEME – *Loving Self & Others: Quieting the Judgments*

Observing wild animals in Africa, a pattern appears in species after species. Dominant males are surrounded by harems of attractive females. Nearby, young males develop their strength and skills hoping to dethrone the king while young females prepare themselves to join the harem. "Rank" in the troop pretty much determines whose DNA will be propagated.

We may be the "smart monkeys," but our concerns are a lot like those of these other mammals. It's no accident that kids in middle school (who are perhaps closest to our simian ancestors) refer to their insults as "ranking" on one another. As adults, we're a bit more subtle, but concerns for how we compare to others still rule our lives.

**Even casual observation reveals that our minds are judgment machines, constantly giving ourselves and others report cards, making comparisons.** For example, do you ever find yourself evaluating who is better liked, earns more money, has the nicer car or home, is more attractive, has the more desirable partner or family, is healthier, smarter, or gets more attention or respect? The list goes on and on.

Do you always win in these comparisons? Me neither. And when we lose, our feelings of envy or inadequacy hurt.

Because our self-critical judgments stem from the same hardwired instincts that impel us to judge others, when this system gets going, everyone loses. When our minds criticize others, it's just a matter of time until we become the target of similar self-criticism. **But if we can find a way to accept others, we automatically receive the gift of self-acceptance. In the end, we find that we can only love others to the degree that we can love ourselves, and we can only love ourselves to the degree that we can love others.**

## COMPASSION PRACTICE FOR THE WEEK

### Letting go of Comparisons

*First reflect on recent moments when your mind made comparisons between yourself and others. Note the qualities or criteria that caught your attention (such as wealth, strength, intelligence, attractiveness, generosity, caring, etc.).*

*Now reflect on why these qualities are important to you. Where did you learn that they mattered? When did you first start using them as criteria to evaluate yourself or others?*

*Finally, imagine what your life would be like if you could fully accept yourself and others, regardless of how they "ranked" according to these criteria. Let yourself try to live with the awareness that judgments don't actually matter.*

## 27

RICHARD C. SCHWARTZ, PhD, chose this quote:

Your task is not to seek for love, but merely to seek and find all the barriers within yourself that you have built against it.

*Rumi (1207-1273)*

## THEME – *Releasing Your Love & Compassion*

Rumi's advice is sage because it implies that the problem isn't that we need to develop the capacity for love and compassion; instead, it already exists within us and our task is to release what is already there, like the sun behind the clouds. To do that he asks us to find the clouds we have built against that inner light. But, if such wonderful capacities already exist inside, why would we build barriers to this essence?

**Opening one's heart involves risking being vulnerable. When we remain narcissistically insulated, fearfully isolated, driven to distractions or to alcohol/ drugs, we can avoid the adventures of the heart that have gotten us hurt in the past.** Most of us have protective parts that share Bilbo Baggins' approach to life that he advocated in the Hobbit, "We're just plain quiet folk and have no use for adventures. Nasty disturbing uncomfortable things, make you late for dinner. I can't think what anybody sees in them."

Suppose we take Rumi's advice and find these protective parts in us, how do we convince them to drop their weapons when it is true that the risks of vulnerability are extremely high? If we care about people, they in turn could abandon, humiliate, or control us. If we weren't so self-involved, we could wind up re-experiencing shame, rejection, anxiety, or other nasty, disturbing, uncomfortable things. Why take such risks?

The answer is that we have to lower the risk in order to achieve more of what Brené Brown calls "shame resilience." It turns out that those uncomfortable feelings are contained by young, vulnerable parts of us that are frozen in past times when we were hurt or shamed and whenever anything similar happens in the present, all those feelings are reactivated and overwhelm us. Once we heal those hurting parts, then vulnerability isn't so scary, the stakes are lower and our protective parts will step down, allowing our inner sun to shine on those around us and on those who suffer around the world. In addition, with that healing, we won't have to spend so much time and energy trying to fill the emptiness or compensate for the worthlessness inside with the accolades of others or with material things, because we will have a stronger sense of our own inherent worth. There becomes more space in our sphere of compassion when it isn't so cluttered by our frantic striving.

*Think of a person to whom have closed your heart.*
*This could be a family member, intimate partner, colleague,*
*anyone you choose. Then, in your imagination, put that person*
*in a room by him or herself, such that you are looking at him*
*or her from outside the room through a window.*

*Now focus on the state of your heart in your chest and notice*
*where it feels closed, calloused, crusted, or congested.*
*Focus on one of those protective feelings and try to open your mind*
*to the part of you that is keeping your heart that way. Ask that feeling*
*what it is afraid would happen if it didn't protect your heart that*
*way and wait for an answer to come, rather than trying to think*
*of the answer. That answer will likely give you a hint regarding*
*the hurt part that it protects, so see if you can show the protector*
*appreciation for trying to protect you that way, and ask if it would*
*be willing to let you get to know more about the hurt part it protects.*
*If the answer is "no," respect that answer and find a therapist*
*to help you with the next steps. If the answer is "yes," ask the*
*hurt part to tell you about itself and why it is so hurt. As it does so,*
*see if you can show it compassion; in other words you are extending*
*love to a younger version of yourself.*

*Simply compassionately witnessing the pain of this hurt part of you*
*will go a long way toward healing it and making you less vulnerable to the*
*person in the room. Then it will be safer to open your heart to him or her.*

# 28

**"**

# True compassion does not come from wanting to help out those less fortunate than ourselves, but from realizing our kinship with all beings.

**"**

*Pema Chödrön*

# THEME – *Widening the Circle of Compassion*

Nearly all of us live with an unrecognized circle drawn around us. It's a circle of compassion. Those beings inside the circle with us receive compassion because there is little distinction between them and us. When my daughter stubbed her toe on the leg of a table the other day, I immediately felt a tightening of my muscles all throughout my body. I grimaced. My shoulders compressed. I didn't *try* to empathize with her – it was just my natural reaction. If she is sick or hurt, my natural reaction is to help her. She's in my circle.

Some people have a very small circle. They're alone and everyone else is outside. For others, their circle includes their immediate family and may include extended family. There are circles defined by the members of one's church congregation or military unit. The mafia has its own circle. So does a professional football team. Your dog that you've had since he was a puppy may be in your circle. Your neighbor's dog probably isn't.

Most of us involved in spiritual practice think of ourselves as relatively compassionate. But how wide is our circle and how are we disbursing compassion? What would we see if we reviewed our compassion statement the way we review our bank statement?

**There are two things we can do. We can work to widen our circle and we can practice with the hope of ultimately dissolving the circle altogether.** Widening the circle involves developing a greater sense of kinship with more and more beings. We can develop this perspective through meditation, *Naikan* reflection, and meditative practices like *tonglen*. That is the inside/out approach. The outside/in approach is to engage more with the world, to get to know people more deeply, to understand the nature of their suffering and their lives, to support them and act compassionately towards them.

The narrowness of our circle gives us a sense of separateness, a sense that true, heartfelt compassion is available only for a select few. Einstein referred to this sense of separateness as a delusion, a prison, and called on us to break free and find our kinship with all living beings.

## *Widening the Circle*

1. *Draw a circle on a sheet of blank paper. Inside the circle write the names of some of the people that are already in your circle of compassion.*

2. *On that same paper write the names of a few people you know that are outside that circle. It can include people from whom you are estranged.*

3. *Pick one person from inside your circle and reflect on your relationship with them. Allow an idea of something you can do for them or something you can give them to naturally arise. Act on that idea within 24 hours.*

4. *On a different day, pick one person from outside your circle. Meditate on that person for 15 minutes using the following questions:*

  a. *What challenges is he or she facing at this point in time?*

  b. *What losses has he or she experienced in the past?*

  c. *What is one example of support or help you have received from this person in the past?*

  d. *What have you done to contribute to this person's suffering (include ways you tried to help that may have caused discomfort or frustration for them)?*

5. *At the end of your period of reflection, contemplate possible acts of support and compassion that you may be able to offer this person. Ask yourself, If this person were in my circle of compassion, what would I do?"*

*Quotes Nº29 to 37*

# A Better Way to Deal With Reactive Emotions: Anger, Hate, Criticism, & Fear

QUOTE #29 – Brach
*A Sacred Pause from Reactivity*

QUOTE #30 – Lokos
*Navigating Fear*

QUOTE #31 – Young-Eisendrath
*Compassion Dispels Hate*

QUOTE #32 – Fields
*Dealing with Anger*

QUOTE #33 – Schwartz
*Hate Blocks Compassion*

QUOTE #34 – Fields
*Being Less Critical of Others – Right Speech*

QUOTE #35 – Saturn
*"Hurt People Hurt People": Transformative Compassion for Difficult People*

QUOTE #36 – Becker
*Responsiveness Instead of Reactivity*

QUOTE #37 – Linehan
*Compassionate Action*

# 29

TARA BRACH, PhD, chose this quote:

❝

# Between stimulus and response there is a space, and in that space lies our power and our freedom.

❞

*Viktor Frankl,* Man's Search for Meaning, *1997*

## THEME – *A Sacred Pause: from Reactivity*

**We spend many of our moments in a trance. Rather than living from a wakeful presence,** we tumble into the future, reacting to the changing array of pleasant and unpleasant experiences. The patterns of our reactivity form a limiting prison — they keep us from the creativity, aliveness and love that express our natural being.

The liberating practice of compassion begins with a pause. In that pause, we begin to notice what's happening — a worried thought, a flash of irritation, a craving for sweets. **With that recognition, we allow what is there to be there, without doing anything. I call this a sacred pause: In these moments of recognizing and allowing life to be just as it is, we enter the space of freedom.** You might try it now. Just stop for a moment, feel what is right here and simply be.

*With practice, compassion practices reveal who we are beyond the limiting story of a separate self.* **Historic patterns of defensiveness and aggression loosen, and the light of our being shines through.** As we inhabit this timeless presence, we naturally respond to the world with intelligence and care, with wonder and joy. *Our lives have power and beauty because we are living from the source.*

## COMPASSION PRACTICE FOR THE WEEK

### *Finding the Space of Freedom*

*At a time when you feel calm, identify and write down several situations where you become moderately reactive — perhaps with anxiety or irritation. Some examples: "Getting my son ready for school," "being caught in rush hour traffic," "approaching a deadline for a project," "feeling fatigued at work," "being criticized by my partner."*

*Select one, and for the next week have the intention to pause inwardly in the midst of this situation. You might outwardly be moving, but discontinue any conversation and step out of your thoughts.*

**In the moment of pausing, the most important thing is to offer a non-judging, friendly quality of attention to your experience.**
*In fact, the friendlier the better! Honor that this is a moment of awakening and, in that spirit, take a real interest in what is happening inside you. Is there tension in your chest? Knots in your stomach? Numbness? Pressure? Are you aware of anger? Anxiety? Craving? What are you believing? Breathe with whatever sensations or emotions are there, and just offer them a respectful, allowing presence.*

*Depending on your situation, this step of pausing and attending to your feelings might take 30 seconds to a minute. Then take a few full breaths, relaxing with each out-breath, and resume your daily activity. Notice the difference between being caught in reactivity, and being awake, here and now.*

## 30

ALLAN LOKOS chose this quote:

## " 

# One of the effects of fear is to disturb the senses and cause things to appear to be other than what they are.

## "

*Miguel de Cervantes,* Don Quixote, *1607-15*

# THEME – *Navigating Fear*

**I believe that the opposite of love and compassion is fear.** Fear is an obstacle to love. Fear is an opponent of compassion, and a formidable opponent at that. Wisdom is seeing things as they really are. Therefore, it would follow that developing a kind and loving heart would help us live more wisely. A useful rule to remember is: **if it looks like wisdom, but is unkind, it is not wisdom; if it feels like compassion, but is not wise, it is not compassion.** Significantly, love and fear cannot be active in us at the same time. In other words, if we are thinking, speaking, and acting from a truly loving place within, we are not experiencing fear. Conversely, **if our thoughts, words, or deeds are motivated by fear, we will not be acting with compassion.** At such moments, we might think that if so-and-so didn't act that way, or if such-and-such hadn't happened, we would be happier, which might be so. But circumstances and conditions are as they are, and it is how we experience them that determine our happiness. Louisa May Alcott apparently understood this when she said, **"I'm not afraid of storms, for I'm learning to sail my ship."**

What most of us want is to be accepted unconditionally for who we are, with our mistakes and unskillfulness. Likewise, we need to accept others for who they are. We need to realize that the wishes, desires, and needs of others are as important to them as ours are to us. To be a loving, compassionate person is to understand that we are all fellow travelers on this journey, that we all experience the joys and sorrows that comprise this adventure called life.

The practice of *metta*, or loving kindness, as taught in the Buddhist tradition, is the offering of loving thoughts first to one's self and then, progressively, to all beings. This practice of offering thoughts of loving kindness can dissolve fear, anger, and greed, which are the saboteurs of love. The ultimate *metta* practice is to become a loving person in even the most challenging and abusive situations. This does not mean becoming a doormat, but rather being one who acts with compassion in any circumstance. **In some of us the seed of love may have gone dormant because it has not received the light, warmth, and nutrients needed for its growth. But love is like the sun: no matter how many cloudy days hide its face it is always there, ready to shine through in the next moment.**

## COMPASSION PRACTICE FOR THE WEEK

*When feeling angry, tense, or anxious, remind yourself that these feelings are grounded in fear. Stop and try to identify the cause of the fear.*

*When you experience impatience, resentment, or anger, stop and ask yourself, "All right, what is this fear?" It can be difficult for some of us to acknowledge fear, but it is an absolutely normal feeling and part of the human condition. Ask yourself again quietly, "What is this fear?" Remember, thoughts, words, emotions, and deeds not coming from love and compassion are likely coming from fear.*

## 31

POLLY YOUNG-EISENDRATH, PhD, chose this quote:

## In this world hate never yet dispelled hate. Only love dispels hate. This is the law, ancient and inexhaustible.

*The Buddha,* The Dhammapada:
The Sayings of the Buddha, *Thomas Byrom, trans., 1976*

## THEME – *Compassion Dispels Hate*

These lines from the *Dhammapada* have always inspired me to remember the core teachings of life: **that only compassion and friendliness allow us to achieve a peaceful way of being.** They are the attitudes that permit us to know ourselves and to know others, especially those whose opinions, views, and ways of life are antagonistic to our own (frequently, these are the people that we live with and are "supposed to love"). The Buddha's words do not imply that we cannot be angry or disagree with one another, but only that **the passion of hatred cannot be dispelled by more hatred.**

When I was a child of twelve, I recall standing in front of a utility sink in the basement of my parents' home and watching a fleeting thought/feeling in my mind's eye: "I hate my father!" This was a kind of awakening. I had not understood why his presence brought me such distress. For example, when he returned to our house at the end of his long workday at the rubber factory, he brought a profound disturbance into the calm, peaceful, and clean environment my mother and I preserved. Exhausted and dirty, he stepped through the door and usually my mother shouted out, "Wipe your feet before you come into the kitchen!" That initiated a line of ragged and raw verbal assaults between them that I can now, decades later, see as their inability to allow any love in the presence of their feelings of intrusion and annoyance about one another. They were very different people, my mother and my father. Each wanted to remake the other in her or his image. But it seemed that my father "brought" this disturbance into the house because it wasn't there until he arrived. And so, when I was a child, I sided with my mother.

I didn't realize I was feeling her feelings that day at the utility sink. I thought they were my own. I felt a deep relief to know that this was the character of "hatred." I had never before felt it for anyone else in my life. On only one occasion did I express my hatred to my father ("I hate you! You are ruining our lives!" I said when I was eighteen and he refused to get up from the bed, where my mother had been waiting on him day and night, because he thought he was dying of prostate cancer even though the doctor had told him many times that he had an enlarged prostate, but not cancer). I felt satisfaction in saying it.

**Over the many years of digesting my hatred for my father, I came to realize that it was made of "love disappointed" and that my hatred could not have existed without the love.** The love was fundamental. I had experienced my father preventing me from feeling the tremendous love that I had felt for him in my youngest years when we were very close. After my mother died, when I was in my fifties (my father having been dead for a couple of years already), I began to feel a deep compassion for my father and to recognize how unfair my mother had been to him.

That compassion released my feelings of love for my father. I have come to regard compassion and love as different experiences although they are related. Compassion opens our hearts as we "suffer with" another. We can open our hearts to strangers – people and animals – whose suffering we witness. I believe that compassion is a natural condition in the human heart because of our original attachment to a mother/other on whom we depend for our own lives. Even a newborn infant can gaze at the face of her mother and attempt to soothe or help the mother. Premature twins who are removed from their mother's womb have been seen to stroke one another's arms to comfort each other.

**Love, as distinct from compassion, means that we can deeply accept another, not wanting to change a hair on the other's head.** We see the other just as he or she is and we accept all of the agitation, hatred, difference, and inconvenience the other has caused us because the love is bigger than its opposite. Compassion can be the conduit to feeling love in the presence of hatred.

## COMPASSION PRACTICE FOR THE WEEK

### Metta *Practice*

*There are many forms of* metta *practice; the one I like best is composed of the following phrases, beginning with my self:*

*May I be happy.*
*May I be free from inner and outer harm.*
*May I find peace.*
*May I find ease in living.*

*I say each phrase aloud at the end of my sitting practice and after I recite a translation of the* Metta Sutta. *After stating each phrase, I spend some moments in silence allowing the phrase to soak in.*

*After saying the* metta *for myself, I repeat the same phrases for my "friends and family." The next round I say for "my enemies and adversaries" and that is where I find my richest insight into compassion. When I think about those people with whom I disagree politically and emotionally, I can see how much they would be helped by happiness, freedom from harm, inner peace and ease in living. I imagine them coming into more warmth and expansiveness and in this way, I can see them as suffering humans just like myself, formulating their opinions and ideals from the ground of their being, just like I do. I imagine all of us relaxing and laughing together – having a picnic. Then finally, I say* metta *for all beings, while holding in mind this warm view of those people with whom I disagree.*

## 32

RICHARD FIELDS, PhD, chose this quote:

**If you get angry easily, it may be because the seed of anger in you has been watered frequently over many years, and unfortunately you have allowed it or even encouraged it be watered.**

*Thich Nhat Hanh,* Taming the Tiger Within, *2004*

# THEME – *Dealing with Anger*

*This quote is important because* **anger blocks connection and goodness**.

Unfortunately anger has been planted or seeded from generation to generation. The habit of responding with anger is reinforced (watered) with each angry incident.

Anger is a difficult emotion to tame because it has some very powerful addictive physiological and psychological reinforcers. You can even find yourself trying to justify your anger because it is hard to control.

I have counseled many people who have suffered significantly, and lost a lot because of their anger and anger related behavior. *The sooner they work on their anger and resentments, and stop blaming others, progress begins.*

The word HALTS stands for being **H**ungry, **A**ngry, **L**onely, **T**ired, **S**ick. It is used to remind the person in alcohol/drug recovery that when they are in HALTS, they are more vulnerable to relapse. You are also more prone to respond with strong anger, when you are in HALTS.

The goal is to not water anger. By not succumbing to anger you slowly weaken it. As time goes on, it becomes easier to reduce your "habit of anger". Rather than having a heavy heart when angry, you can instead have an open heart and practice goodness of heart, self-compassion and compassion for others.

If you do get angry, don't beat yourself up about it. It is a lapse, which is normal, and it means there is more work to be done.

## COMPASSION PRACTICE FOR THE WEEK

### *Reducing Anger*

*This week focus on reducing your anger. Recognize when you are
in HALTS and act accordingly by trying to wait until you are
out of HALTS to deal with issues. Recognize what sparks your anger.
Notice how frequently you have little flare-ups of emotion or anger.
See how well you do at recognizing your "hot buttons" (e.g. money issues,
politics, relationship issues, bad drivers, etc.) Resist feeding these
anger flare-ups, so the fire of anger is not sparked.*

## 33

RICHARD C. SCHWARTZ, PhD, chose this quote:

I imagine one of the reasons people cling to their hates so stubbornly is because they sense, once hate is gone, they will be forced to deal with pain.

*James Baldwin*

## THEME – *Hate Blocks Compassion*

Compassion requires that you open your heart to the suffering of others. But what if opening that door to your heart means having to re-experience the pain from your past that you locked away when you closed that door? **Many people keep their hearts closed with hate, judgment, greed, paranoia – all the emotions that block compassion –** because they so fear being overwhelmed by their own hurt if they were to care about someone else's. Instead, they have contempt for their own vulnerability, their sensitivity, empathy, and their neediness. They blame those qualities for getting them hurt in the first place and vow to never again be so weak.

If you cannot afford to care about the parts of you that are suffering, then it's hard to care about people who suffer in similar ways. **If you hate your vulnerability, you will have contempt for those who show theirs.**

When this is true, compassion-building practices alone will not make a lasting difference. **People need to heal their inner pain so that opening their hearts is not so threatening.** They need to compassionately witness what happened to them in the past so as to unload the burdens that make them harden their hearts. Short of that, whatever compassion they feel will be forced and short-lived.

## COMPASSION PRACTICE FOR THE WEEK

*Spend some time considering all the different reactions you have regarding vulnerability in yourself or in someone else.*

*When you start to feel sad, hurt, weak, needy, or ashamed, how do you react? That is, are you critical of yourself for feeling that way? Do you distract yourself from that state as soon as possible? Do you hide that vulnerability from others or feel shame if you show it?*

*When you see someone acting hurt, weak, needy, or ashamed, how do you feel toward them? Is there a part of you that is contemptuous of them, that is glad you're not them and comes up with reasons why you wouldn't be like them? Do you feel uncomfortable in the presence of their vulnerability and try to get away from them as soon as possible?*

*The point of this exercise is not to bring you more shame as you become aware of the substantial obstacles to the release of your natural compassion. The point is to provide a starting point for transforming these obstacles.* ***Approach with curiosity and compassion these protective parts of you that keep your heart closed to your pain and the pain of others. If you can witness and heal the suffering parts, you won't have to work so hard to be a compassionate person. You will just be one.***

## 34

RICHARD FIELDS, PhD, chose this quote:

66

The thought manifests as the word;
The word manifests as the deed;
The deed develops into habit;
And habit hardens into character.

So watch the thought and
its ways with care
And let it spring from love,
Born out of concern for all beings.

99

*The Buddha*

## THEME – *Being Less Critical of Others: Right Speech*

The Buddha reminds us that the cycle of criticism starts with the critical thought. You can look at being critical of others as a thought disorder, and something that requires a more compassionate touch.

*Being critical of others distracts us from being present and having an open heart.*

When you are critical of others, that could be a signal that you are upset with yourself. So it is better to just work on yourself.

A parody of the Alcoholics Anonymous serenity prayer says this well.

> *"Grant me the serenity to accept the people I cannot change,*
> *Courage to change the one I can,*
> *And the wisdom to know it's me."*
>
> *Anonymous*

### COMPASSION PRACTICE FOR THE WEEK

*If you find you are being critical, slow down, stop and*
**refocus on being more concerned, caring and compassionate.**

*The third path of the Buddhist eight-fold path is "right speech".*

*It is said that words can help create peace or wars, invoke compassion or hatred, affirmation or shame, join or divide, love or destroy. Right speech involves words of honesty, kindness and nurturance. Right speech involves speaking only what is worthy and valuable.*

*Guidelines for right speech involve telling the truth, speaking gently with warmth and friendliness. Mindful or right speech is described as "aesthetically" pleasing like a work of art.*

*This week practice right speech to counter criticism.* **Metaphorically see yourself playing a harp in harmony with others, rather than wildly and erratically slamming the drums of criticism.**

## 35

SARINA SATURN, PhD, chose this quote:

# If we learn to open our hearts, anyone, including the people who drive us crazy, can be our teacher.

*Pema Chödrön*

## THEME – *"Hurt People Hurt People":*
## *Transformative Compassion for Difficult People:*

It is easy to open our hearts to those who have showered us with love, affection, and support. Conversely, it can be quite difficult to open our hearts to those who have caused us aggravation, sadness, and pain. We are emotional creatures and evolutionarily designed to pay attention to and remember the people who bring us well-being, as well as those who cause us harm. Thus, it is natural to adhere to the bearers of goodness and avoid the deliverers of badness. **However, it is important for us to recognize our shared humanity. Everyone has struggles, triumphs, hopes, and fears.**

The most intolerable people we encounter can turn out to be our greatest teachers. How can this be? **They can teach us about ourselves: buttons to push, areas of sensitivity, and patterns of insecurity.** They can also teach us about others: the ways in which judgment, ignorance, lack of exposure, and acting out of negative emotions can cause injury. This brings to mind the old adage that proclaims, **"Hurt people hurt people." Indeed, people who lash out and wound others are often times experiencing deep anguish themselves.**

To grow compassion within ourselves, it is essential to plant the seed of understanding so that we may grow to love everyone, including those who seem very unlovable at times. These difficult people may need our love most of all. When we begin to understand where others are coming from, and how they came to be the way they are, **we will come closer to finding peace within ourselves by finding liberation from the shackles of resentment and remorse. It is transformative to cultivate a compassionate, forgiving, open, and loving heart for all people, including cherished ones, objectionable ones, and ourselves.**

### COMPASSION PRACTICE FOR THE WEEK

*Sit down in a quiet place, place your hands over your heart,
and practice mindful breathing for several inhales and exhales.*

*First, bring to mind a person whom you love deeply. Think of
a very tender moment you have shared with this individual
and feel the affection flow through your body. Reflect on the warm
feeling this recollection brings to you. Then, think of a difficult moment
that occurred with this person – perhaps an argument, misunderstanding,
or hurt feelings – and think about how you moved through this
conflict and still hold this person very dear despite this bump
in the road. Think of how this person has taught you about your
capacity for compassion and love. Now turn back to the caring moment
you shared and allow the gratitude and kindness to wash over you:*

*May you experience abundant compassion.*
*May you find forgiveness for yourself and others.*
*May you discover gratitude for the lessons taught to you by others.*
*May your pains and sorrows soften.*
*May you feel our shared humanity.*
*May you find peace and love in your heart.*

*Next, think of someone who drives you crazy. This may be*
*a relative, co-worker, friend, acquaintance, or a stranger who did*
*something to really bother you. Reflect on what this person may have*
*experienced in order to act in ways that hurt you. Perhaps his or her*
*upbringing, genes, stressors, environment, and/or suffering caused*
*this person to rub you the wrong way.* ***Realize that this person is***
***also one of your greatest teachers:***

*May you experience abundant compassion.*
*May you find forgiveness for yourself and others.*
*May you discover gratitude for the lessons taught to you by others.*
*May your pains and sorrows soften.*
*May you feel our shared humanity.*
*May you find peace and love in your heart.*

*Finally, turn to yourself. Reflect on all your great qualities,*
*including your capacity to love and forgive. Realize that you too have*
*hurt others in the past and that we are all human. Move back to*
*holding yourself in the light with self-compassion. Radiate good*
*wishes for everyone in this world, including yourself:*

*May I experience abundant compassion.*
*May I find forgiveness for myself and others.*
*May I discover gratitude for the lessons taught to me by others.*
*May my pains and sorrows soften.*
*May I feel our shared humanity.*
*May I find peace and love in my heart.*

---

# 36

**"**

If someone comes along and shoots an arrow into your heart, it's fruitless to stand there and yell at the person. It would be much better to turn your attention to the fact that there's an arrow in your heart...

**"**

*Pema Chodron,* Start Where You Are: A Guide to Compassionate Living

## THEME – *Responsiveness Instead of Reactivity*

Who among us hasn't experienced an arrow to the heart? It's so painful! And it is an inevitable experience in human relationships. Isn't it tempting to react by blaming them, or otherwise shooting an arrow right back into their heart? Slinging arrows at each other when we are hurt tends to make our relationships more painful, less safe, and feeds a downward relational spiral. It's definitely a common human impulse, but it isn't a particularly skillful action to take. Things usually end up worse, instead of better. Hurting others doesn't help our wounds to heal, it just increases the likelihood of being further injured because it perpetuates injury.

In order to move from a place of reactivity to responsiveness we need start by disengaging from reactivity. We can pause and anchor ourselves in the sensation of the breath (or other sensations if the breath is problematic for us). In doing so we create the possibility of a more stable awareness.

Next we turn our attention to ourselves. What is it that is triggered in us, and what is it we are needing? When we see our own injury fully, turn toward ourselves and the pain that we feel, we can understand the nature of the injury and begin to explore what is needed to tend to the pain in our own injured heart. Sometimes it is difficult to know what we need. In this case it may be helpful to consider what we would say and do for a dear friend who was injured in the same way. Might we treat ourselves with the same kindness and compassion?

Tending to our own needs with kindness and tenderness, creating the conditions **for the healing of our own heart, is a much more skillful response. If we can remember to pause and take the time to tend to our own healing, we can engage in relationships from a position of wholeheartedness.**

### COMPASSION PRACTICE FOR THE WEEK

*To tend to ourselves we begin with the* **STOP practice***:*

**S- Stop.** *Remember to pause. We begin breaking through reactivity by slowing down, pausing, and making space for something new to happen.*

**T- Take a breath.** *Actually, take a few breaths. Let everything else rest in the background as you privilege your awareness on the sensation of breathing. Anchoring our awareness in the breath gives us the chance to anchor in this moment and this body.*

**O- Observe.** *What is happening here in this moment, and this body? Notice the thoughts, emotions and sensations present. No need to change them in any way.*

*Just notice them. Allow the attention to broaden*
*a bit to fully take in what is happening right now.*
*Given your new perspective, perhaps asking yourself,*
*"What do I need right now?"*

**P- Proceed to Practice.** *Now that you have a better*
*understanding of what is happening, and what you need,*
*see if you can find a way to honor your needs.*
*Perhaps pausing was all you needed, or maybe you need*
*to take a walk, have tea, sit in meditation.*
*Maybe there are some words you need to hear. What would*
*you say to a dear friend in the same situation?*
*Can you say those to yourself now? The point is to give*
*ourselves what we need to move out of the state of reactivity,*
*to comfort, soothe and reassure ourselves and move into a*
*state of responsiveness. Tending to our true needs, rather than*
*reacting from whatever place was triggered in us is the key.*

## 37

ROSHI MARSHA LINEHAN, PhD, chose this quote:

**"**

# It is not enough to be compassionate. You must act.

**"**

*His Holiness the Dalai Lama, 2008*

# THEME – *Compassionate Action*

The Oxford English Dictionary gives several definitions of compassion. "Suffering together with another," and "the feeling or emotion, when a person is moved by the suffering or distress of another, and by the desire to relieve it," are two such definitions. Both definitions leave out the actual act of doing something to relieve the suffering of the other.

When you are the one suffering, compassion alone is simply not enough. Georges Bernanos, a French novelist and political writer, said, "I know the compassion of others is a relief at first. I don't despise it. But it can't quench pain, it slips through your soul as though a sieve." This sums up my thoughts exactly. **Wanting to help another is simply not sufficient. Finding ways to do it, learning what we need to know to relieve the suffering of others, developing the skills to be effective – these are what matter at the end of the day.**

When I was a supervisor, I once rebuked a supervisee for reinforcing a client's sense of her own helplessness. The therapist had felt the distress of her client to such a degree that she almost immediately reached out and swept away the event causing the client so much pain. After the rebuke, it was clear my student thought I had no compassion.

So I told her the following story: "Imagine a person is standing in hell, standing on coals on fire, jumping up and down and screaming, 'Help, help, bring me some water and pour it on my feet! I can't stand this. I am burning up.'" Then I asked her who she thought was most compassionate – the person who runs to get a pitcher of water and climbs down into hell to pour the water on the poor soul's feet, or the person who rushes down to hell, gets behind the poor soul and pushes, saying, "Let's get out of here."

Her answer was remarkable. "Marsha," she said, "the difference between us is that you think you can get people out of hell." Her response was very important because if it were true that she could not help get people out of hell, then she was correct – pouring water would be the wise thing to do.

A year or so later, the therapist called me to thank me. She had learned skills that allowed her to give up on clients less easily in the service of teaching them how to get out of hell.

This story illustrates my passion for evidence-based treatments. It is all too easy to provide a compassionate ear to those in hell. We feel better ourselves and, at times, listening brings temporary relief to the other person. It is undoubtedly better than no relief and occasionally it may really be all that we can offer. But what if we took the time to learn more effective ways to help? What if we learned the evidence-based treatments that are out there for the learning? What if we insisted that others learn them, not to avoid suffering one client's pain with them, but to add actions that are known to help? Would not that be the more compassionate response?

*The compassion practices that go with this story are two-fold.*

**First**, *when listening to others in pain, it is important to be mindful of not only the other person's suffering, but also of our own.*

*Mindfulness of current emotions and sensations is important because through it we learn that indeed we can tolerate both our suffering and that of others. Breathe in and notice sensations of emotion. Breathe out and notice sensations of emotion. Noticing, allowing, in and out.*

**Second** *is the practice of "wise mind." Remind yourself that each of us has the capacity for universal wisdom. Though it may be difficult to reach, it is possible. Breathe in deeply, let your mind drop to your center; listen to the silence within, listen in the depth of the emptiness that is itself wisdom. Breathing in and out normally, letting yourself settle into wisdom itself, asking, and, at times, questioning; listening for an answer (but not answering). Breathing in, breathing out, dropping into the silence.*

*Quotes №38 to 42*

# Opening Your Heart: Kindness, Generosity, & Forgiveness

QUOTE #38 – Halifax
*Kindness: The Grace of Compassion*

QUOTE #39 – Goldstein
*Being Kind Whenever Possible*

QUOTE #40 – Phillips
*Radiating Loving Kindness*

QUOTE #41 – Salzberg
*The Power of Generosity*

QUOTE #42 – Brach
*Practicing Forgiveness*

# 38

ROSHI JOAN HALIFAX, PhD, chose this quote:

**"**

# Kindness is the grace of compassion.

**"**

*Anonymous*

## THEME – *Kindness: The Grace of Compassion*

Someone once told me that **kindness is the grace of compassion**. It is one of the ways we express our love and nonduality in relation to each other. Kindness is a quality of great value for our work on behalf of those who are suffering. **How can we give care without kindness? Of course, kindness needs to be there, or our care is cold and mechanical, defensive or shrunken with fear, tentative and distracted.**

## COMPASSION PRACTICE FOR THE WEEK

*This practice is from the Tibetan Buddhist tradition. The practice is*
*so simple, and yet may be one of the hardest things we can do.*
*It is a practice of ultimate and extreme compassion, a brave act of love*
*when we see through the eyes of another.*

*First remember why you are practicing.*

*Recall your aspiration for this vow to really be of benefit to others,*
*for this vow to awaken you from your own suffering.*

*Let your practice rest in the hands of your good heart*
*as you remember your innermost request.*

*Now, bring to your mind and heart the presence of someone*
*who is suffering deeply. Maybe this one is sitting before you now.*

*Open your heart and mind to this one.*

*Feel your way into this one's heart.*

*Look out through his or her eyes.*

*Really imagine that you are this person, living their life,*
*feeling their suffering, and knowing this one's heart.*

*Be this one.*

*Feel into how they experience their world, their life.*

*Exchange yourself for this one.*

*Spend time being this one.*

*After some time has passed, let yourself rest in unconditioned presence.*

*End the practice by dedicating the merit to the well-being of others.*

## 39

ELISHA GOLDSTEIN, PhD, chose this quote:

"

# Be kind whenever possible. It is always possible.

"

*His Holiness the Dalai Lama*

## THEME – *Being Kind Whenever Possible*

When we look at this quote we have to really ask, is it really always possible to have compassion? When someone cuts you off on the highway or another person has 14 items in the 10 items or less express line, is kindness possible? Or how about when we're feeling particularly stressed, anxious, or depressed, is compassion even possible then? Or when someone is abusive toward you?

**Many would argue that the doorway to happiness is to a life geared toward kindness and compassion.**

However, compassion does not mean that you have to agree with what someone is doing or even be tolerant of it. Accepting verbal or physical abuse is certainly not compassionate toward yourself.

Fundamentally, we need to learn how to be kind to ourselves. Many of us find that the most difficult practice of all. That is why in the practice of cultivating compassion, we begin with ourselves.

More often than not when I ask people all the things they have to do that day, there is a long list. When I then ask, "And where are you on this list?" a quizzical facial expression forms as if I were speaking a tongue from another planet. Whatever the reason, we're just not kind to ourselves and that makes it difficult to spread that kindness to others.

Compassion is often contagious and if a few more of us were infected by it, we would have more nurturing environments at home, work, and in public places.

The bottom line is that compassion is considered a strength in many traditions, including the field of psychology. It can also be nurtured formally and through little acts during the day.

So is it always possible? Well, we can hold that as an aspiration or as the light to guide our intention. **However, if it is too difficult sometimes, don't pressure yourself too much. Just come back to it when you can with intention and notice how you feel overall.** Most of all, don't just take the Dalai Lama's word for it, try it out for yourself and see how it goes.

## COMPASSION PRACTICE FOR THE WEEK

*Making Compassion Part of Daily Life:*

*Set an intention for today to look for moments where you are aware of either yourself or another suffering.*

*In that moment, ask yourself if it is possible to respond with kindness. If so, act with kindness.*

*See how you feel after the act is completed. At the end of the day, we always want our experience to be our teacher.*

*As you intentionally practice and repeat it, you'll notice more moments of grace like this falling in on you throughout the day.*

# 40

JENNY PHILLIPS, PhD, MSN, chose this quote:

**"**

A human being is a part of the whole, called by us 'Universe,' a part limited in time and space. He experiences himself, his thoughts and feelings as something separated from the rest, a kind of optical delusion of his consciousness. This delusion is a kind of prison for us, restricting us to our personal desires and to affection for a few persons nearest to us. Our task must be to free ourselves from this prison by widening our circle of compassion to embrace all living creatures and the whole of nature in its beauty. Nobody is able to achieve this completely, but the striving for such achievement is in itself a part of the liberation and a foundation for inner security.

**"**

*Albert Einstein*

## THEME – *Radiating Loving Kindness*

This beautiful quote is particularly stunning for me because it reflects the wisdom of a Western scientist rather than an Eastern spiritual teacher. Perhaps it is because of my near total lack of understanding of mathematics and Einstein's theory of relativity, but I did not expect a Nobel Prize scientist to have such sentiments! When I encountered this quote, I found it expressed with such haunting beauty the deep experience of inter-connectedness. You can sense that it is based upon direct experiential awareness rather than formulaic reasoning.

**Metta, or loving kindness, means to radiate out from a constricted focus on the "Self" as separate from the "Other," from "Me" and "Mine" to "Us" and "Everyone." What a huge task this is for us to achieve! It requires persistent practice, working against our biological nature.**

Ironically, our spiritual nature is often most available during times of threat, crisis, and suffering rather than times of good fortune and material plentitude. I have marveled at this after many years of working with prisoners who often live under dire and dangerous conditions. Their minds are ready to explore the most fundamental existential issues of survival, peace, and happiness. In the midst of this deepened awareness of self, they can expand their circle to others.

My concern is that the world is rapidly becoming more distracted and self-centered. As prisoners like to say, **"The only way out is in."** This wisdom gained from those within the belly of the beast of incarceration can remind us to practice loving kindness.

## COMPASSION PRACTICE FOR THE WEEK

*Sit in a comfortable position. Let your mind be still. Focus on the breath. Hold an image or sense the presence of all those to whom you are sending selfless love and good wishes. Feel the* metta *coming from your heart and moving forth into the universe.*


*May all beings be filled with loving kindness.*
*May all beings be well.*
*May all beings be peaceful and at ease.*
*May all beings be happy.*

# 41

66

# If you knew as I did the power of giving, you would not let a single meal pass without sharing something.

99

*The Buddha*

## THEME – *The Power of Generosity*

**Generosity is a matter of spirit. It has little to do with whether or not we have material goods to give or don't.** There is always something that we can give to another, for giving is our heart's offering of connection and caring.

In India and Burma I was the recipient of incredible generosity from many people who had very little materially to offer. Yet when they gave, they did so wholeheartedly. People there taught me about generosity, and showed me that it doesn't depend on conventional, external abundance. And if we cannot offer something material, we can give energetically: a smile, or our full, undistracted attention.

The Buddha said that no true spiritual life is possible without this kind of generous heart. Generosity is the very first quality of an awakened mind because of the beautiful quality of joy that arises in an act of true giving. Giving is a happy thing to do. We experience happiness in forming the intention to give, in the actual act of giving and in the recollection of the fact that we have given. Generosity has been one of my own important personal practices because it reminds me of the capacity of my own heart to go beyond fear ("What if I need that book next week? What if I'm not giving enough?") to honor the power of connection.

### COMPASSION PRACTICE FOR THE WEEK

*This is a practice that helps cultivate generosity through awareness:*
*If a strong impulse to give something arises in your mind*
*and it won't cause any harm (like giving away your family's rent money),*
*then make the offering. Stay aware of what is arising in your mind,*
*especially if the next fifty thoughts following the intention*
*to give are fearful, like: "Maybe I'll wear it next year";*
*"Maybe I will read it after all"; "What if they think*
*I'm stupid for doing this?" Let the thoughts go*
*as you remember your motivation, and remember*
*that **generosity is actually a practice, one that implies***
***intentionality, challenges and venturing into new terrain.***
*Stay aware of your thoughts and feelings after the act of generosity.*
*Are you in fact regretful? Relieved? Buoyant?*
*Let your insights guide your ongoing practice of generosity.*

# 42

**"**

# Our failure to know joy is a direct reflection of our inability to forgive.

**"**

*Charlotte Joko Beck*

## THEME – *Practicing Forgiveness*

Forgiveness is a wonderful idea — until we really have something to forgive. When we have been betrayed and wounded, when we are threatened and afraid, holding onto resentment is a way of protecting ourselves. It is our way of armoring against the experience of raw pain.

Consider where you might be carrying resentment or blame. What would happen if you stopped believing your story of someone being wrong or bad? What's the most difficult thing you'd have to experience? *For most of us, when we put down our story of wrongdoing, we are forced to feel our powerlessness and vulnerability, our hurt and fear.* There's a good reason we hold so tightly to our hatred and anger. Yet we have an inner wisdom that intuits the suffering inherent in an unforgiving heart. In a movie called *The Interpreter* (2005), this wisdom is expressed in a short phrase:

## *"Vengeance is a lazy form of grief."*

Vengeance is also a lazy form of fear and hurt. *It is "lazy" in the sense that it's easier to lash out than to feel our suffering.* Yet ultimately this aggression does not serve us. We have to bring presence to our wounded heart if we are to heal and live fully. In the words of Zen teacher Charlotte Joko Beck, **"We forgive for the freedom of our own hearts."** Forgiving doesn't mean that we become passive in the face of harmful behavior. It may be that we forgive but dedicate ourselves to never letting that harm happen again. We may forgive but maintain very strong boundaries to protect ourselves or others. *Forgiving simply means that we are unwilling to put another person — or ourselves — out of our heart.*

Forgiving is a lifetime practice. We regularly close and tighten against others, and we are often at war with ourselves. Yet we can learn to recognize when we've constricted and then to connect with our intention to forgive. Our sincere intention alone begins to open the door. The full process of forgiving may require the support of healers, therapists and friends, or we might do it alone. Either way, gradually we'll find that we are letting go with increasing ease. *We are more at home in an undefended heart, a heart that is free to love without holding back.*

*Scan your life and identify and list those people toward whom
you are carrying resentment. For a week, or as long
as it takes, select one of these people and let your intention be
to loosen the mental habit of blame.*

*When you become aware of blaming thoughts, pause.*
**Without any self-judgment, become curious about what lies under blame.**
*Ask yourself: If I had to let go of this resentment, what unpleasant
feelings would be there? Feel your body and sense what is true.
Is there fear, self-blame, powerlessness? In these moments, simply bring
a compassionate presence to whatever is arising in you.*

**What is your experience of yourself when you shift from blaming
another person to a kind presence with your own experience?
What is the quality of your heart? Your awareness?**

**Remind yourself that releasing blame and resentment is the
pathway to an unconditionally loving heart.**

# SECTION
# VII

*Quotes N⁰ 43 to 52*

# Compassion
# & Suffering

## 43

FRANK OSTASESKI chose this quote:

**"**

How far you go in life depends on your being tender with the young, compassionate with the aged, sympathetic with the striving and tolerant of the weak and strong. Because someday in life you will have been all of these.

**"**

*George Washington Carver*

## THEME – *Turning Toward Suffering*

Compassion arises as an intelligent and appropriate response from our being in the presence of suffering. There is no shortage of human suffering in our world so it is reasonable to ask if compassion arises as a response to suffering and there is so much suffering, why isn't there more compassion? Perhaps it is because we so rarely allow ourselves to actually face and touch the suffering directly. We are masters of distraction.

Healing is always found by going toward suffering. A common misunderstanding of compassion is that you should help someone feel safe; to help him or her feel there is no danger. This is fine of course, if you can do it, but in my hospice work I have seen that for many, dying does not feel safe. However, **when I am compassionately present, the patient begins to trust and be open not because there is no danger, but because they sense an attunement, felt as support, which enables them to go toward the suffering**.

Compassion expresses the gentleness, the kindness necessary for our heart and our soul to relax and to trust. Without the presence of compassion we cannot fully open to suffering. Often the presence of compassion heals a particular pain right away. But sometimes the presence of compassion allows us to stay with what might otherwise be too difficult to tolerate. By staying with the experience of suffering, compassion allows a deeper truth to be revealed.

**It seems that the real significance of compassion is not exactly about removing suffering, it is about cultivating our capacity to be with suffering.** This increased tolerance for suffering allows us to set down our defenses. When our defenses are down we can look objectively to see the actual causes of suffering. Then we can act skillfully to help remove those causes.

## COMPASSION PRACTICE FOR THE WEEK

*Consider each of the following questions:*
1. *What is a way that you try to avoid suffering?*
2. *How do you experience compassion?*

*Use journaling, contemplation, or open-ended inquiry
to discover what is true. Sense the body, feel the heart
observe the mind. Track and report what is occurring
as it occurs. Release yourself from the habit of knowing
or the pressure of censorship. Simply respond to
the questions spontaneously, truthfully, and compassionately
from a place of curiosity. It can be helpful to repeat
the questions to notice how your responses change. Let yourself
experience the impact of your answers.*

## 44

ELISHA GOLDSTEIN, PhD, chose this quote:

66

# Don't turn away. Keep your gaze on the bandaged place. That's where the light enters you.

99

*Rumi, 13th-century Sufi poet*

## THEME – *Being with Suffering*

In one of my favorite quotes, Rumi points to a universal truth of healing: **The way to emotional freedom is through being with and embracing that which is painful or difficult in us rather than trying to fix, push away or run from it.**

Now, there's nothing wrong with trying to fix things. Without this ability, you wouldn't have the seat you're sitting in, the computer you're looking at or the clothes you're wearing (if you're wearing them). Most of the time we're not even aware we're trying to avoid things.

However, when it comes to our emotions, trying to think our way out of them is only a path of avoidance. This avoidance creates further suffering.

Think about it for a second. What happens when you try and think about becoming less anxious or depressed? You go up into your head and start swirling around about why this is happening and maybe what you can do about it. In other words, **we add stress to discomfort.**

It is in the very moment that we become intimate, in a nonjudgmental way, with our discomfort that we send the message internally that we care about ourselves ("the light enters you"). This begins to transform the moment.

## COMPASSION PRACTICE FOR THE WEEK

*When you experience an uncomfortable feeling,*
*try this experiment for a single minute:*

*"Breathing in, I feel this feeling; breathing out, I let it be"*

*You can shorten this to just saying*
*"feel" on the in-breath and "let be" on the out-breath.*

*The instructions are simple, but the practice may not always be easy.*
*Be kind and gentle with yourself through this process.*

# 45

> ❝
>
> When one door
> of happiness closes,
> another opens, but often
> we look so long at the
> closed door that we do not
> see the one that has been
> opened for us.
>
> ❞

*Helen Keller,* We Bereaved, *1929*

## THEME – *Seeing Opportunities & Possibilities*

This quote deeply humbles me. A woman who was both blind and deaf, Helen Keller changed the world because of — not in spite of — her disabilities.

Life is in a constant state of flux and change. This means that we will inevitably lose things we dearly love, whether they are people, objects, or hopes and dreams. **It also means that we will gain the unexpected, and that we will be presented with undreamed of opportunities for love, growth, and discovery.**

When we only focus on what we have lost, however, or what we want but don't have, we often don't notice these opportunities. We miss what is right beneath our noses. But there is a silver lining to almost every cloud, a truth to which most people can attest.

## COMPASSION PRACTICE FOR THE WEEK

*Here's a practice that can help you see possibilities and not just problems in life. First, think of one or two of the biggest challenges you've faced in your life so far, problems that were so difficult you thought you'd never get through them at the time. In hindsight, can you see if anything good came out of the experience? Did you grow as a person, learn something important, find more meaning in your life, develop a new relationship? If you could, would you go back in time and change what happened if it meant that you wouldn't be the person you are now because of it?*

*Now think about a challenge you're facing right now. Are there any positive things that might come out of your present circumstances — any learning opportunities, career possibilities, new relationships, ways to re-organize your priorities?* What is life trying to teach you right now? *Is there any way that this seeming curse might actually be a gateway to a beautiful new adventure?*

*For the next week, try to intentionally reframe any difficult or challenging experiences in this way, and see what happens!*

# 46

CHRISTINE A. COURTOIS, PhD, ABPP, chose this quote:

So how do you sit with a shattered soul? Gently, with gracious and deep respect. Patiently, for time stands still for the shattered, and the momentum of healing will be slow at first. With the tender strength that comes from an openness to your own deepest wounding, and to your own deepest healing. Firmly, never wavering in the utmost conviction that evil is powerful, but there is a good that is more powerful still. Stay connected to that Goodness with all your being, however it manifests itself to you. Acquaint yourself with the shadows that lie deep within you. And then, open yourself, all that is you, to the Light. Give freely. Take in abundantly. Find your safety, your refuge, and go there as you need. Hear what you can, and be honest about the rest: be honest at all cost. Words won't always come; sometimes there are no words in the face of such tragic evil. But in your willingness to be with them, they will hear you; from soul to soul they will hear that for which there are no words.

*Kathy Steele*, "Sitting With the Shattered Soul," Pilgrimage: Journal of Psychotherapy and Personal Exploration, *1989, 15 (6), p. 24*

## THEME – *Compassionate Prescence*

I chose this quote because I have been taken with it for many years and often use it at the end of treatment workshops. I also included it at the end of my book *Healing the Incest Wound* (2010). Kathy Steele is a friend who has long inspired me in my work with trauma survivors. She models her philosophy and her quote captures her compassion and the spiritual dimension and respect needed to work with the traumatized.

**The lesson is to sit quietly, join the person, be patient, and listen. Witness and be present and attuned in order to break through what is often the excruciating isolation and wordless silence of the trauma survivor.** Your presence will communicate respect and compassion, even when there are no words. This is especially important when the trauma is interpersonal and has created a chasm of mistrust between self and others. Compassionate presence is, in and of itself, healing.

## COMPASSION PRACTICE FOR THE WEEK

*Sit quietly in a centered way, using your breath to quiet you. Once you are calm, focus on what it means to have a shattered soul. Allow yourself to resonate and empathize with those who have been shattered. Open your heart and mind to the suffering involved. Send your energy and kindness and know that you do not need words to be with them.*

*Gently end the practice when you are ready and let yourself know you can make a difference by witnessing and by caring.*

## 47

DIANE POOLE HELLER, PhD, chose this quote:

> Wounding and healing are not opposites. They're part of the same thing. It is our wounds that enable us to be compassionate with the wounds of others. It is our limitations that make us kind to the limitations of other people. It is our loneliness that helps us to find other people or to even know they're alone with an illness. I think I have served people perfectly with parts of myself I used to be ashamed of.

*Rachel Naomi Remen*

## THEME – *The Gift of Compassion & Trauma Recovery*

The lesson I find here is finding the" hidden gift" in Trauma – that when it is integrated, understood and a at least partially healed, it expands us. Afterward, we will never be the "normal" self we once were before it happened. Trauma forces us to stretch beyond what we thought possible, much like giving birth. Ask any woman if she ever thought having a baby physiologically possible.

Trauma tears us apart and when we come back tougher again, we are new, more improved, more compassionate and caring, less petty, less self-absorbed and more attuned to the suffering of all humanity, – not just the singularity of our own. This gift is best discovered by the client themselves as there is an organic time and place. When we have taken a deep dive into our own suffering and come out stronger, we have the capacity to meet our clients in their darkest places. We are simply willing to "BE"; to show up in PRESENCE; to midwife the beauty of the mess that is real healing.

## COMPASSION PRACTICE FOR THE WEEK

### *Reversing Role Reversal toward Restoring Secure Attachment*

### Part One

*Imagine one of your parents or grandparents (alive or deceased) in your mind's eye and connect with them from the inside.*

*What do you feel their life is like?*

*What do they love, and what do they long for?*

*What do they need right now in this imaging?*

*What might it be like for you to see them with many competent, caring adult resources?*

*Perhaps you see them with family that knows how to support them well or with friends that know to connect and to love them. Or their partner is affectionate and attentive with them and they come home with flowers and they dance away the evening in your living room.*

*Can you see them having these needs met well?*

*What do you see they need?*

*Which adult(s) know/s how to provide that need?*

*Who can be with them in an honoring, authentic, compassionate way?*

## Part Two

*What happens in your body, heart or mind when you see them satisfied in this imagining (even if it was not like that in your childhood – especially if it was not like this in your childhood?)?*

*What difference does it make to see them loved and well – with adult resources and support?*

*What happens in you now? Do you feel less burdened or more able to feel carefree or have a sense of the possibility of a more pleasurable, less worried childhood?*

*What difference does it make when they have other adults to rely on who are happy to be available to them?*

*It is suggested that you repeat this exercise each day this week, with different family members.*

---

# 48

DONALD MEICHENBAUM, PhD, chose this quote:

## "

# Opportunities to find deep powers within ourselves come when life seems most challenging.

## "

*Joseph Campbell*

## THEME – *"Post Traumatic Growth": Resiliency & Compassion*

When really bad things (traumatic events) happen to good people, such as the experience of natural disasters, serious accidents, life-threatening illnesses, and exposure to violence – such as terrorist attacks, combat, and sexual victimization – people are usually impacted in the immediate aftermath. However, most individuals (some 75%) evidence resilience, or the ability to bounce back from, adapt to, and overcome such ongoing adversities. In fact, some individuals, families and communities evidence **"post-traumatic growth."** It is not as if these individuals do not also at times experience strong emotional reactions, since post-traumatic distress and resilience can co-exist. **Joseph Campbell's quote reminds us that challenges can bring out our best qualities.**

In contrast, some 25% of victimized individuals will evidence ongoing distress, adjustment difficulties and, in some instances, persistent psychiatric disorders such as Post Traumatic Stress Disorder (PTSD), depression, anxiety, and alcohol/drug abuse and dependence.

Among the many things that distinguish these two groups of 75% versus the 25% are the nature of the "stories" that they tell themselves and that they share with others. Resilient individuals are able to view themselves as moving from being "victims," to being "survivors," and even "thrivers."

Resilient individuals are able to be more compassionate toward themselves and toward others. Compassion, as well as other positive emotions like optimism, gratitude, perseverance/grit, and forgiveness can facilitate the recovery process.

## COMPASSION PRACTICE FOR THE WEEK

*Envision a good friend or favorite relative who is in the same situation as you. He or she has come to you for help. Think about ways you could listen non-judgmentally and WITH COMPASSION.*

*What would you say?*
*What would you do?*

*Could you use the same understanding, kindness, warmth, and support toward yourself that you would offer your friend or relative?*

**Can you introduce your "Compassionate Self" to your "Suffering Self"?**

*Think about ways to move forward without self-blaming, self-criticizing, and stress-engendered behaviors.*

**You are in charge of your rate of progress, your journey to resilience and personal growth.**

*Can you begin to "restory" your life?*

## 49

RICHARD FIELDS, PhD, chose this quote:

66

# I am the source of most of my suffering because of the habits of my own mind.

99

*His Holiness the Dalai Lama*

## THEME – *Self-Induced Suffering*

This quote reminds us how we create and perpetuate our own suffering. It is purported that at the age of eight, while reciting the four noble truths, the young Dalai Lama was told by his teacher that he was reciting with too much ego. The young prodigy reflected on this, and then uttered this insightful remark.

How often do you allow your thoughts to ruminate to the point where a situation and feelings escalate? You might find yourself magnifying problems, escalating emotions, and creating problems that don't exist. You can also make things worse by blaming yourself or others for this pattern of self-induced suffering.

**The habit of ruminating about past interpersonal injustices, as well as, having high expectations of others, limits relationships in the present. The result is often feelings of isolation and disconnection that cause more suffering.**

Reducing the intensity and depth of this self-induced suffering is possible by putting things in a compassionate and mindful perspective. A perspective that can be achieved by learning to soften, quiet, and relax your reactivity.

### COMPASSION PRACTICE FOR THE WEEK

*Whenever you find yourself being reactive, with feelings of anger, criticism, blame, and fear, you can use the breath to calm your body and mind.*

*Sit in a comfortable setting and focus on slow in and out-breaths. On the in-breath take in the reactive emotions. On the out-breath slowly release these emotions. Do this for several breaths. On your next in-breath, take in your criticism and blame of self and others. On the out-breath release the criticism and blame. Continue this practice for several cycles of in and out-breaths.*

*Now, close your eyes and imagine a cloudless and expansive blue sky. Bring into consciousness the beauty and gentleness of this blue sky. Perhaps a few birds are flying and circling overhead. Maybe they are hawks soaring on the thermals. Notice their seemingly effortless ability to glide both lower and higher, with great skill, ease, dexterity, and grace.*

*Imagine yourself being able to metaphorically fly above it all, breathimg in the fresh air, while feeling the calming warmth of the sun. Realize how expansive and beautiful life can be. Let the gentle breezes calm you, as the feelings of anger, criticism, blame and fear subside.*

## 50

PAUL GILBERT, PhD, chose this quote:

**"**

# If I let you get to know me I might reveal things about me that you don't like and then I'll feel shame and I will be with somebody who doesn't really like me but must be nice to me.

**"**

*Typical Client Fear*

## THEME – *Shame & Compassion*

I have heard this sentiment many times in therapy, especially when working with high-shame clients. People have all kinds of reasons for not letting others get too close and for not letting in compassion. The fear of being shamed is a main one.

Carrying shame within us can stop us from being compassionate with ourselves. Research has shown that some people really struggle with being open, accepting or responding to compassion from others, or even noticing it, and that many struggle with self-compassion and treating oneself kindly, especially in the context of mistakes or setbacks. There are many reasons for this.

A major fear of letting others get to know us is linked to the fear of allowing them to see what's going on in our minds. Our brains are constantly generating all kinds of fantasies, complex emotions, and intrusive images. We can have the feeling that some of these must never be known and that if people really knew what went on in our minds, we would become objects of shame and rejection.

**Compassion for aches and pains and losses is doable. Compassion for the things that cause us shame is much more difficult. Yet we know that it is love and compassion that heals us; it is feeling accepted and forgiven that is the most powerful process of change within us. Compassion is a great healer of shame – we need to allow it in.**

## COMPASSION PRACTICE FOR THE WEEK

*The first meditation is to spend a few moments considering that everything that goes on in our mind, no matter what it is, it is part of being human. Our genes and our life experiences have shaped our brains to give rise to these inner experiences. This is not our fault. The more we understand this, the more compassionate we can be toward ourselves and others as we realize that we are all following the arising and flow of created desires and emotions for good or ill.*

*As we become mindful and observant of the mind, we become aware that this is not just "my mind" but the mind of nature – that is, as we observe the flow of thoughts and emotions like anger, worry, anxiety, sexual and other desires, we are observing "a human mind" at work; a mind created by nature. So the first step is to not overly personalize the contents of our minds but to see them as part of our common humanity and of "nature's mind."*

## 51

RICHARD FIELDS, PhD, chose this quote:

"

# All beings want to be happy, yet so very few know how. It is out of ignorance that any of us cause suffering for ourselves or for others.

"

*Sharon Salzberg,* Lovingkindness:
The Revolutionary Art of Happiness, *1995, p. 78*

## THEME – *Happiness & Compassion in Lieu of Unhappiness (Dissatisfaction) & Self-Blame*

**In our striving for happiness we fuel our fear of unhappiness** and, in so doing, we lose sight of happiness and joy in our present, moment to moment life.

We often see joy and happiness as something we will attain in the future. We delude ourselves in thinking that when we have enough money, the right job, the right relationship, the right car and house, the right family situation, then we will be happy. In striving for these things we can lose sight of the happiness and joy available to us in the present moment. We forget to breathe and live life, and enjoy each moment, each breath. The Dalai Lama says it well: **"If you want others to be happy, practice compassion. If you want yourself to be happy, practice compassion."**

### COMPASSION PRACTICE FOR THE WEEK

*When you are in what I call a "grumpy" mode with feelings of discouragement, frustration, and dissatisfaction, it is hard to have gratitude or even acknowledge the good things in your life. Anger and fear have replaced happiness and compassion, especially compassion for oneself.*

*You can shorten your time in "grumpy" mode*
*by not personalizing situations,*
*reducing expectations of others,*
*letting go of feelings of inadequacy and shame,*
*disputing distorted realities,*
*and accepting all feelings, including dissatisfaction.*

*You can stop suffering and begin to feel compassion for yourself. You can be more present, enjoying life more and being more compassionate towards yourself and others.*

*List those things, people, and situations that bring you happiness.*

# 52

SYLVIA BOORSTEIN, PhD, LCSW, chose this quote:

> ## May all beings, omitting none, feel safe and content and happy, and live with ease.

*The Metta Sutta*

**THEME – *The Metta Sutta: A Compassionate Wish for the Well-Being of All***

It has been my experience from the start of my career as a psychologist that therapists practicing across the spectrum of therapies agree that **the essential healing element in all therapeutic collaborations is the sense of being truly seen**. I believe that even more healing than the sense of being seen is the conviction that someone wants to see us and is willing to suspend preconceived ideas, views, and opinions in order to do that.

Seeing people as people just like myself, without preconditioned stories, allows me to remember that everyone suffers and delights, just as I do, in this ever-challenging life and evokes in me empathic responses of compassion or joy that do not depend on particulars. I would like to be able to wish, as the *Metta Sutta* instructs, "May all beings, omitting none, feel safe, and content, and happy, and live with ease." To the extent that I can "see" others on this intimate level, I will feel supported by my own natural benevolence.

We haven't as a species, gotten there yet, but maybe we will. **We are wired, I believe for compassion, so I am hopeful that we can achieve that connection.**

### COMPASSION PRACTICE FOR THE WEEK

*This last compassion practice reminds us
to practice the* Metta Sutta's *theme of compassion for all beings:*

*May all beings, omitting none, feel safe, and content,
and happy, and live with ease.*

# Appendix

■

*Contributors*

■

*Photo Credits*

■

**Richard Fields, PhD, Editor**     *QUOTE NOS. 10, 26, 32, 34, 49, 51*

Richard is the founder/director of FACES Conferences (www.facesconferences.com), the mission of which is to bring mindfulness and compassion training to mental health professionals.

He has over thirty-five years experience specializing in outpatient alcohol/drug relapse prevention and recovery. He is the author of the college textbook, *Drugs in Perspective*, 9th ed. (2016).

He is also the author of *Awakening to Mindfulness* (2008) and is the editor of *A Year of Living Mindfully* (2012) and *A Year of Living with More Compassion* 1st Edition (2013), 2nd edtion, (2016). He also maintains a private mindfulness and compassion coaching practice.

**Michelle Becker, LMFT**     *QUOTE NO. 36*

Michelle is in private practice in San Diego utilizing a mindfulness and compassion based approach to psychotherapy. She is a certified teacher of Compassion Cultivation Training, and Mindful Self-Compassion, with a particular interest in how mindfulness and compassion can enhance relationships.

**Sylvia Boorstein, PhD, LCSW**     *QUOTE NO. 52*

Sylvia is cofounding teacher of Spirit Rock Meditation Center. She is the author of five books on Buddhism, mindfulness, and meditation. She is the author of *Happiness Is An Inside Job: Practicing for a Joyful Life* (2008).

**Tara Brach, PhD**     *QUOTE NOS. 17, 29, 42*

Tara is a clinical psychologist, internationally known meditation teacher and author of the bestselling books *Radical Acceptance*, and *True Refuge*. Tara's podcast addresses the value of meditation in relieving emotional suffering and serving spiritual awakening, and receives over a million downloads each month. In addition to her public teaching, she is active in bringing meditation into DC area schools, prisons and to underserved populations.

**Christine A. Courtois, PhD, ABPP**     *QUOTE NO. 46*

Chris has retired from clinical practice in Washington, DC. She co-authored *Posttraumatic Stress Disorder*, and has received the American Board of Professional Psychology, 2016 Distinguished Service Award to the Profession of Psychology.

**Chris Germer, PhD** *QUOTE NOS. 1, 21*
Chris is a Lecturer on Psychology, Part-time at Harvard Medical School. He is the author of *The Mindful Path to Self-Compassion* (2009) and coeditor of *Wisdom and Compassion in Psychotherapy* (2012) and *Mindfulness and Psychotherapy*, 2nd edition (2013).

**Paul Gilbert, PhD** *QUOTE NOS. 3, 50*
Paul is head of the Mental Health Research Unit as well as Professor of Clinical Psychology at the University of Derby, United Kingdom. He has been developing compassion-focused therapy for people with high shame and self-criticism. He is currently a series book editor for *Compassionate Approaches to Life Difficulties* with New Harbinger (USA) and Constable Robinson (UK).

**Elisha Goldstein, PhD** *QUOTE NOS. 14, 24, 39, 44*
Elisha is co-founder of the Center for Mindful Living in West Los Angeles, CA. He is the author of many publications including *Uncovering Happiness*. He and his wife, Stefanie Goldstein, PhD., are co-designers of the 8-week program CALM – Connecting Adolescents to Learning Mindfulness.

**Roshi Joan Halifax, PhD** *QUOTE NOS. 16, 38*
Joan is a Buddhist teacher, anthropologist, author, and social activist. She is the Abbot and head teacher at Upaya Zen Center in Santa Fe, NM. She is the author of many books, including *Being with Dying* (2008).

**Diane Poole Heller, PhD** *QUOTE NO. 47*
Diane is an expert in the field of Adult Attachment Theory, Trauma Resolution, and integrative healing techniques including working with Somatic Strategies and the Relational Field. She has created the Dynamic Attachment RE-Patterning experience and the DARe to CONNECT series. She is a renowned trainer, presenter, and speaker.

**Jack Kornfield, PhD** *QUOTE NO. 18*
Jack is an internationally renowned meditation teacher and one of the leaders in introducing Buddhist practice and psychology to the West. Trained as a Buddhist monk in Thailand, Burma, and India, he is the co-founder of Spirit Rock Center in northern California. He is the author of many books including *A Path With Heart* (1993) and *The Wise Heart* (2008).

**Gregg Krech** *QUOTE NO. 28*
Gregg is a leading expert in Japanese Psychology and the Director of the ToDo Institute in Vermont. He is the author of *Naikan: Gratitude, Grace, and the Japanese Art of Self-Reflection* (2002) and *A Natural Approach to Mental Wellness* (2011) (www.todoinstitute.org).

**Roshi Marsha Linehan, PhD**  *QUOTE NO. 37*
Marsha is Professor of Psychology, Director of the Behavioral
Research & Therapy Clinics, Univ. of Washington, and author of
*Cognitive-Behavioral Treatment of Borderline Personality Disorder* (1993).

**Allan Lokos**  *QUOTE NOS. 19, 30*
Allan is the founder and guiding teacher of The Community
Meditation Center in NYC. He is the author of the best seller *Patience:
The Art of Peaceful Living* (2012) and *Pocket Peace: Effective Practices for
Enlightened Living* (2010).

**Michael Meade, D.H.L.**  *QUOTE NO. 9*
Michael is a renowned storyteller, author and scholar of mythology,
anthropology, and psychology. He combines hypnotic and fiery
storytelling, street savvy perceptiveness, and spellbinding interpretations
of ancient myths with a deep knowledge of cross cultural rituals.

Michael is the founder of Mosaic Multicultural Foundation, author of
*Fate and Destiny, The World Behind the World,* and *The Water of Life.* For
more information, about Mosaic and Michael, visit www.mosaicvoices.org.

**Donald Meichenbaum, PhD**  *QUOTE NO. 48*
Don is a Distinguished Professor Emeritus from the Univ. of Waterloo,
Ont., Canada. He is a recipient of a Lifetime Achievement from
the American Psychological Assn. He has published extensively and
his most recent book is *Roadmap to Resilience* (2012)
(www.roadmaptoresilience.org).

**Bill Morgan, PsyD**  *QUOTE NO. 12*
Bill is a clinical psychologist in private practice in Cambridge and
Quincy, MA. He is a founding board member of the Institute for
Meditation and Psychotherapy He has led mindfulness retreats for
mental health professionals for the past 20 years. He is a contributing
author of *Mindfulness and Psychotherapy* 2nd edition. His book, the
*Meditator's Dilemma* was recently published by Shambhala.

**Kristin Neff, PhD**  *QUOTES NOS. 2, 4, 8, 13, 45*
Kristin is a pioneer in the field of self-compassion research and the
author of *Self-Compassion* (2011). She is an Associate Professor of
Human Development, Culture & Learning Sciences at the Ed. Psych.
Dept. of the Univ. of Texas at Austin.

**Frank Ostaseski**  *QUOTE NO. 43*
Frank is a Buddhist teacher, founder of the Metta Institute, and
co-founder of Zen Hospice Project, the first Buddhist hospice in
America. He is one of America's leading voices in contemplative
care of the dying. Frank can be reached at www.mettainstitute.org.

**Jenny Phillips, PhD, MSN** *QUOTE NO. 40*
Jenny is the author of *Letters from the Dhamma Brothers: Meditation Behind Bars* (2008) and the producer of the award-winning documentary film *The Dhamma Brothers*. Jenny has a private practice in Concord, MA. She has a new film being released – *Beyond the Wall* (beyondthewallfilm.com)

**Diane Poole Heller, PhD** *QUOTE NO. 48*
Diane is an established expert in the field of Adult Attachment Theory, Trauma Resolution, and integrative healing techniques including working with Somatic Strategies and the Relational Field. She is a renowned trainer, presenter, and speaker. She has created the Dynamic Attachment Re-Patterning experience and the DARe to CONNECT series on healing early childhood and adult attachment wounds.

**Sharon Salzberg** *QUOTE NO. 41*
Sharon is one of America's leading meditation teachers and writers. Her most recent book, *Real Happiness* (2010), is a New York Times Bestseller. She is also author of *The Kindness Handbook: A Practical Companion* (2008), and *Lovingkindness: The Revolutionary Art of Happiness* (1995).

**Sarina Saturn, PhD** *QUOTE NO. 35*
Sarina is an assistant professor at the University of Portland, Portland, OR. She received her PhD in neuroscience from NYU and was a postdoctoral fellow at the Univ. of California, Berkeley, CA. Her current research investigates the biology underlying prosocial emotions.

**Richard C. Schwartz, PhD** *QUOTE NOS. 20, 27, 33*
Richard is the developer of the Internal Family Systems (IFS) model of psychotherapy and the president of the Center for Self Leadership, which coordinates training programs in IFS around the world (selfleadership.org). He has written 4 books and over 30 articles or chapters on IFS.

**Shauna L. Shapiro, PhD** *QUOTE NOS. 5, 7, 23*
Shauna is a professor at Santa Clara University, a clinical psychologist, and an internationally recognized expert in mindfulness. She has published over 150 articles and book chapters, and is the co-author of the critically acclaimed texts, *The Art and Science of Mindfulness*, and *Mindful Discipline*.

**Daniel J. Siegel, MD** *QUOTE NO. 15*
Dan is the Executive Director of Mindsight Institute. He is a Clinical Professor of Psychiatry at the UCLA School of Medicine, and Co-Director of the UCLA Mindul Awareness Research Center.

He is the author of *The Developing Mind; Pocket Guide to Interpersonal Neurobiology; The Mindful Therapist; Mindsight*; and *The Mindful Brain*. He is co-author of *Parenting from the Inside Out* (with Mary Hartzell), and of *The Whole-Brain Child* (with Tina Bryson).

**Ronald D. Siegel, PsyD** *QUOTE NOS. 11, 26*
Ron is Assistant Clinical Professor of Psychology, Harvard Medical School and serves on the Board of Directors and faculty of the Institute for Meditation and Psychotherapy. He is the author of *The Mindfulness Solution: Everyday Practices for Everyday Problems* (2010) and coeditor of *Mindfulness and Psychotherapy*, 2nd. ed. (2013).

**Stan Tatkin, PsyD, MFT** *QUOTE NO. 22*
Stan is a clinician, author, developer and co-founder of the PACT Institute. He teaches at UCLA, maintains a private practice in Southern California, and leads PACT programs in the US, and internationally. He is the author of *Wired for Dating, Wired for Love, Your Brain on Love*, and co-author of *Love and War In Intimate Relationships*.

**Amy Weintraub, MFA, ERYT-500** *QUOTE NO. 6*
Amy is a pioneer in the field of yoga and mental health for over 20 years. She is the author of the best-selling *Yoga for Depression* (2004) and *Yoga Skills for Therapists* (2012). She is the founder/director of the LifeForce Yoga Healing Institute (www.yogafordepression.com).

**Polly Young-Eisendrath, PhD** *QUOTE NO. 31*
Polly is a psychologist, writer, speaker and Jungian analyst. She has published 15 books her most recent, *The Present Heart: A Memoir of Love, Loss and Discovery*. She maintains a clinical and consulting practice, and is a Professor of Psychiatry at the University of Vermont, and clinical Supervisor at Norwich University.

# Photo Credits